# A Fire to Be Kindled

# A FIRE
## TO BE
## KINDLED

How a Generation of
EMPOWERED LEARNERS
Can Lead Meaningful Lives and
Move Humanity Forward

# Kelly Smith

**LIONCREST**
PUBLISHING

Hardcover ISBN: 978-1-5445-2975-2
Paperback ISBN: 978-1-5445-2974-5
Ebook ISBN: 978-1-5445-2973-8
Audiobook ISBN: 978-1-5445-2976-9

# Contents

# Introduction

You'd think it would be easy to choose a title for a book. After all, the average nonfiction book has 50,000 words; after all that writing, how hard could it be to add a couple more words and print them in large type on the front cover?

For me, choosing the title was tricky. You see, I believe some things that most people don't believe, about humans and learning and our astonishing potential. These ideas can seem trivial or obvious at first glance, but I see profound power and also terrifying danger in them. As a result, any short title I pick can seem both tediously generic and ignorantly optimistic.

But the ideas in this book are real, based on my direct experience helping tens of thousands of children learn. I'm not talking about listening to lectures or memorizing facts; this is learning that leads to real impact for real people. I've seen children go from crying in a parked car, begging their parents not to make them go to school, to literally running to school each morning and complaining about not being able to meet with their class on Saturdays. And it's not only kids: I've seen adults overcome decades of conditioning to become powerful learners.

## So What's with the Title?

You might not spend a lot of time thinking about learning. Maybe you vaguely associate learning with school and place it in the category of "been there, done that." Or maybe you tinker with learning in the context of hobbies or talents, but you enjoy the process too much to count it as learning. Perhaps you've thought about going back to school for a degree or credential, or considered a certification program available through the company you work for.

This book is going to make the case that we consistently underestimate the power of learning. By a LOT.

To clarify, let's go back in time to the words of the ancient Roman philosopher Plutarch:

*"The mind is not a vessel to be filled, but **a fire to be kindled.**"*

This quote is a thousand years old but just as relevant today as ever. It speaks to an important truth about humans. Look closely, and you can see two competing metaphors for the human mind.

The first metaphor is a vessel being filled. Imagine pouring water into a cup. It's a simple process. If I hold the pitcher and tip it, a stream of water pours down into the cup. Same thing, every time.

It's tempting to adopt this paradigm in learning, to the point that I hear seasoned educators use the imagery of pouring knowledge into the minds of their students. If I plan the right lessons and cover all the standards, learning is inevitable. Unfortunately, it's just not the way the human mind works.

Now consider Plutarch's second metaphor: kindling a fire. Have you ever tried to start a fire without matches and lighter fluid? It's a delicate operation. Do you have a way to create sparks? Are the right materials in place to catch the sparks? Are they dry and laid out in a way that gives the right mix of fuel and oxygen? Starting a fire can take hours of struggle. When it works, it feels like a miracle. And as long as the conditions are right, the fire will keep burning!

If you've never started a fire this way before, google the scene in the movie *Cast Away* where Tom Hanks's character, marooned alone on a desert island, finally achieves ignition. He's been desperately, almost maniacally, rubbing sticks together, delicately protecting the sparks. You can feel his genuine exultation in the fire he kindled.

I believe Plutarch was right. The correct way to think about the human mind and our propensity for learning is as a fire to be kindled. It's more chaotic, more challenging, and more uncertain than pouring water into a cup. But it's also uniquely human, special, even sacred. It's what we are meant for. It's sheer power.

Choosing the right metaphor is imperative. Imagine spending all that time and energy to catch a few precious sparks, carefully protecting them from the wind and hoping for a fire, only to start pouring water on it! The wrong paradigm leads to the wrong approach and exactly the opposite result from what we intend.

Seeing the mind as a fire to be kindled is the first step to becoming an empowered learner, which leads to the life of meaning and contribution that we all want. As you'll see in the chapters that follow, it's not obvious or easy to orient your life around learning. It requires discomfort and effort and invariably includes painful setbacks and failures. It always involves other people, which means you will experience the fickleness of human nature. It can run into direct opposition from your local culture, which may punish the learner and set limits on the power of the mind.

But even with these obstacles, I'll argue that there is no better way to live. Learning is core to who we are as humans. It's what we are meant for. We'll all be better off if we choose a life of active learning.

## The Most Powerful Resource

I believe the potential of human beings—and specifically the ability of our brains to learn—is the most powerful resource on the planet. It's a resource that never runs out, but rather multiplies as we get better at learning. This shows up in the long view of history, from tools and fire and the wheel and language, to the printing press and democracy and the airplane and the internet. Humans have a well-documented knack for figuring things out and sharing what we learn so that the next person doesn't have to start from the beginning. Isaac Newton called this "standing on the shoulders of giants." Collective learning may be the most important thing humans do.

Learning in an individual way means food on the table, personal development, and hopefully some fun along the way. But learning as a collective, with others, is a force multiplier with the promise of exponential improvement.

Looking forward, the ability of humans to learn will be the distinguishing factor in the future we experience.

Just as our ancestors faced existential threats like predators, disease, and starvation, we have major challenges today, and our children and grandchildren will face scary problems. Climate change, pandemics, social unrest. At a deeper and more important level, human beings are struggling to find meaning and purpose like never before, underscored by a global mental health crisis, an opioid epidemic, and alarming suicide rates. Even the less extreme drains of zombie-like social media consumption, sugar-laden food consumption, trivial obsession with celebrities, sedentary lifestyles, binge drinking, and a host of other "buffers" are enough to give pause.

As a species, are we unlocking the potential impact of our brains? Are we learning at the level we're capable of? Are we on a clear course to a better, brighter future?

If you're like me, this is a difficult question to answer. On the one hand, there are many stories of humans achieving great things—breakthrough works of art, vaccines invented in a year, momentous acts of forgiveness and love. But it's hard to ignore the pettiness, distractedness, complacency, and all the other foibles that stand between humanity and our inspiring destiny.

Even at the personal level, most of us can point to flashes of inspiration and steps toward greatness, tempered by fears, doubts, insecurities, discouragement, and downright laziness.

My claim—and my reason for writing this book—is that individual lives and the entire human species will be better off if we make a concerted effort to embrace learning as a way of life.

## Learning Is Personal

Before I have any chance of convincing you to care more about learning, it might make sense to share a little bit more about me. The first thing you should know is that I am on a mission to empower learners. I founded an education company called Prenda that helps people run microschools for K–8 students. The mission is, literally, to "empower learners." I try to be an empowered learner myself, and I spend a lot of time thinking about the mindset and behaviors that lead to powerful, transformative learning.

But I wasn't always obsessed, or even aware of the concept. In fact, I discovered it by accident.

For the majority of my life, I held the belief that school and learning were the same thing. School is where you learn; learning happens at school. It's a common mistake. In the 180 years since Horace Mann came back from Prussia with a model for "universal, non-sectarian, free" schools, American parents have gradually come to accept a false premise: send your kids to this government building, and thirteen years later they will emerge with the knowledge, skills, and attributes to be successful and happy.[1]

I was good at school. I made it a game to get the grades and test scores I wanted with minimum effort. I was salutatorian in high school, cum laude in college, and ended up in a nuclear physics graduate program at the Massachusetts Institute of

---

[1] Ellwood Patterson Cubberley, *The History of Education: Educational Practice and Progress Considered as a Phase of the Development and Spread of Western Civilization* (Project Gutenberg, 2005), electronic edition, https://www.gutenberg.org/ebooks/7521.

Technology, where I abruptly understood that school wasn't going to come easily anymore. It was painful to realize that I had not learned the skills I needed to succeed in graduate level physics. Even scarier, I saw that over all those years of succeeding in school, I had not learned ***how to learn***.

Fast forward to 2013. I had left MIT with a master's degree and embarked on a career in technology. I had worked for small and large clean-tech companies, doing engineering, product management, and marketing, and I had recently sold a pre-revenue startup I founded with a friend and taken a job at the acquiring company. Working remotely from my home in Arizona, I thought it was a good time for my eight-year-old son to learn some computer programming. When he was a baby, we sat together at my laptop and made silly games on a tool called Scratch.[2] Now that he was older, he was ready to code on his own.

We could have made it a father–son activity at home, but I figured it might be more fun to invite the neighborhood. After all, computer programming jobs were high-paying and in high demand, so maybe—just maybe—one of these kids would get into coding and find a great living doing something they enjoyed. Mostly, I just thought it would be fun, so after the librarian gave me permission to use the empty computer lab on the second floor of the Mesa Public Library, I designed an ugly poster, printed a dozen copies, and taped them to light poles and street signs in the surrounding neighborhood.

When I ran that first Code Club at the local library, I had no idea of the path I was embarking on. I found myself experimenting with the learning process, ruling out some approaches through trial and error, and locking onto some things that really worked. Kids wandered in off the street. They came back week

---

[2] https://scratch.mit.edu/.

after week and brought their friends. Parents drove their kids thirty minutes across town. The kids loved it, and they were learning in astonishing ways.

I was at Code Club every week for five years. I roped my friends into the project, and it became a community, a nonprofit, and eventually a social impact business, where we provided the tools and training for libraries all across the country to run Code Club programs of their own. Even though the business never made much money, Code Clubs reached more than ten thousand kids, from Queens, New York, to Wister, Oklahoma. It was invigorating to personally engage with thousands of young people, getting a front-row seat to real learning. It was humbling to work with hundreds of adult librarians who cared so much about kids that it didn't matter that they had no prior experience in computer programming. It was exciting to get real-time feedback in a highly engaging learning environment, which I eventually realized had become my personal learning laboratory. I was learning about learning.

Over time, I got to know the kids. Many of them were struggling in school. Some were getting bad grades. They thought they were dumb. They'd tell me they were not good at math. Some had behavior issues. But I had seen these kids code. They were solving hard problems and demonstrating spectacular creativity. The problem, I realized, was not with these kids' brains. I had watched them learn. They were capable of anything. So why was traditional school such a challenge for them?

Meanwhile, I was watching my own children experience formal schooling. They attended the A-ranked public school in our suburban neighborhood, received a steady flow of positive reinforcement in the form of good grades and glowing teacher reviews, and seemed to be gradually losing the natural curiosity with which they entered the world. The fire was going out.

What was going on?

I started asking questions…

*Why do the same kids hate school and love Code Club?*

*What is happening in this afterschool program that is not happening at school?*

*What if school were able to empower learning at this level?*

*What would the structure look like if learning were the goal?*

*How would lives be different? How would the world be different?*

These questions led me to open a microschool. The goal was simple: create a learning environment where kids cultivate the mindset and skills of lifelong learners. I had seen it happen in the afterschool coding program at the library. Could the same engagement happen in my home, with a small group of students learning math, language arts, science, and social studies?

Before I knew it, I was meeting every day with seven kids around my kitchen table. One of them was my own son. Others were children of lifelong friends, and some were more recent connections I had met through Code Club. Some were academically advanced; some were struggling to catch up. Over the course of that first semester, I witnessed a change: each of these kids shifted from passively receiving an education to actively learning.

The microschool concept quickly spread, from the original seven students in my house to thousands of kids from Arizona to New Hampshire. We knew students and their parents were looking for options and hungry for a new approach to education that centers on learning. What we didn't realize in those early days was the vast army of potential learning guides—amazing adults embedded in every community, passionate about helping kids learn, and ready to play a major role as coaches and mentors. Prenda finds those people and helps them run world-class microschools for small groups of students in their neighborhoods.

Prenda's mission is to empower learners, and that happens in microschools all over the US. But the shift to empowered learners is not limited to school-aged children. It's available to everyone, regardless of where you were born, how old you are, and what your affiliation with a formal education institution is. You can be an empowered learner. Having seen the results firsthand, I can tell you that it's worth the effort.

This book will show you how. We'll start with a deeper look at what it means to be an empowered learner, and why it's so rare in today's world. The five chapters after that will explore the inward beliefs and guiding principles of an empowered learner, focused on Prenda's five core values that are celebrated and lived not only by the employees but by the learning guides, students, and everyone else in our community. For each of these core values, I will share a short example from Prenda's experience reinventing education. Watch for these vignettes between chapters. After exploring the core values, I'll finish with one chapter that ties the concepts together in a practical way, with a few warnings and some actionable advice for becoming an empowered learner.

By the time you finish this book, you'll have a deep understanding of the paradigm shift to active learning. You'll see what it looks like through the stories of others, and hopefully you'll see it in yourself. My invitation to you is to look at your life through the lens of learning. What would be different if you approached every challenge with a Figure It Out mentality? Are you talking yourself out of big goals because you doubt your abilities? Do you question whether you can gain the knowledge and skills that will take you where you want to go? Do you wish you had the audacity to be the person you want to be? Deep down, do you wonder if the raw abilities, natural gifts, and unique opportunities bestowed upon you could be developed and improve the world around you?

If that's you, you're not alone. You can be an empowered learner. Keep reading to see how you can experience the thrill of kindling a fire, for yourself and everyone around you. Ready to start?

# Chapter 1

# The
# Empowered Learner

ON THE WALL OF MY OFFICE HANGS A GIANT PRINT OF ONE OF MY favorite photographs. It was taken in 1903, so it's the old kind of black and white, almost sepia tones. The setting is a flat, sandy beach in North Carolina. There are no geographic features of interest, just light gray sky and slightly darker gray ground.

Centered in the photo is a forty-foot-wide airplane. It's clearly "old school," with double canvas wings held up by a skeleton of flimsy wooden poles. There's the faint blur of a spinning propeller. You can make out the shape of a human, lying face down in the middle of the airplane like a modern teenager in a planking competition.

And if you look closely, you can see a tiny distance between the airplane and the ground. That's right; this is a pivotal moment in the course of human history—the first powered flight. Orville Wright is piloting the Flyer and his brother Wilbur is running alongside.

This moment was pure magic. It captures the majesty of human spirit in a way that is hard to describe. Instead of just watching the birds, humans could join them in the sky, and the world would never be the same.

But you've heard all about this story. You probably answered multiple choice questions about it on a history test at some point. You may have read a biography, or seen something on the History Channel. You might have marveled at the ingenuity and resolve of Orville and Wilbur Wright, affirming their well-deserved place in history and, at the same time, writing them off as a different species that has nothing to do with you and your life.

What would you say to someone who invited you to be like the Wright brothers? Does it feel impossible? Ridiculous? Audacious? Hubristic? Insane?

Before you write it off, let's look at the events leading up to that day in 1903, and the continuous iteration and effort over the years that followed. By focusing on six key adjectives, we can see that there's more to the story than meets the eye.

- **Intentional.** Orville and Wilbur studied weather patterns carefully before choosing Kitty Hawk in the Outer Banks of North Carolina. It was the middle of nowhere, but it had ideal wind conditions and soft sand for landings. Each year, they took a train 700 miles from their home in Dayton, Ohio, packing crates of prototype equipment and supplies.

- **Incremental.** The brothers took an estimated 1,000 glides in unpowered devices for three years leading up to the moment in the photo. That track record involved many minor crashes, including scratches, broken bones, and a dangerous wreck just three days before their famous success.

- **Innovative.** When the brothers realized commercial engines were too heavy, their friend Charlie Taylor built a new one. When they figured out that boat propellers were inefficient in the air, they designed a new one and tested it in a home-made wind tunnel.

- **Unsung.** All the attention and hype around powered flight at the time was focused on a guy named Samuel Langley, who had the resources of the Smithsonian and the War Department behind him. No one cared about the Ohio brothers and their experiments in Kitty Hawk.

- **Unimpressive.** With a strong headwind, the actual ground speed of the first flight was 6.8 miles per hour. That's a number that shows up on my treadmill, and I'm not a fast runner. The total distance of that flight was 120 feet, easily within the range a ten-year-old can throw a baseball.

- **Unfinished.** Later that day, after a series of longer flights, a gust of wind flipped the Flyer and damaged it beyond repair. The brothers couldn't fly again until the following year. They had to go back to Dayton and build another model. And in the years that followed, Orville survived another seven major crashes.

When I look closely at the story of Orville and Wilbur Wright, I don't see mythical demigods playing out their destiny as members of a superior species. I see human beings doing the very thing that humans do best: learning.

The story feels like magic because we tell it wrong, skipping over the crashes and challenges, fast forwarding through the boring parts where they spent countless hours tinkering in the shop and looking like madmen to the handful of bystanders in the Outer Banks. We see that they had a big dream, and then in the next breath we tell the story of them achieving their dream.

But it's the middle part—the part we always skip—that places Orville and Wilbur solidly in the category of "humans like me," and it's where the real magic happens. Day after day, month after month, year after year, they *learned*. In this case, they learned something no human had ever learned before. They learned how to fly.

Look closely at the story of anyone you admire, from Martin Luther King Jr. to Mahatma Gandhi; Nelson Mandela to Marie Curie. Unwind their journeys, and you'll notice that each of these "personages of historical significance" was human, including all the foibles that go with it. Not one of these pivotal lives began with a clearly defined recipe for success. Each had setbacks, detractors, and moments of doubt. They set big goals and went after them. Invariably, this means they had to learn. No one has the knowledge and skills they need to achieve any big dream when they start as babies.

The same holds true for people who have accomplished great things but are not chronicled in history books. Has a coach or teacher ever had a life-altering impact on you? Is there a family member you look up to? Has an artist inspired you with their work? Anyone you revere as great may very well be that, but they are also ordinary people, flaws and all. They decided they wanted to do something and they *learned* everything they needed to make it happen.

Anyone can become the type of learner that Orville and Wilbur Wright were. History and our everyday lives are scattered with these learners. They are living meaningful lives and making meaningful contributions, whether you've heard of them or not.

You can be this type of learner, what we'll call an *empowered learner*. It requires effort—both the inward work of transforming core beliefs and the outward struggle of persistence in the face of disappointment. It's not easy, but I can promise that it's worth it.

## Learning Is Power

There's an approach called "first principles thinking" that phys-
icists use to simplify complex ideas. The idea is to cut through
the complexity of a concept and distill it to the most basic
explanation, pulling from the basic rules that are always true.
If you apply this approach to the complicated topic of human
learning, you might arrive at this simple equation:

$$Learning = Power$$

To help this sink in, let's try a thought experiment where we
travel forward in time, say 100 years from now.

Close your eyes. Picture what life might be like in that future
world. Think of somebody living where you live and around your
age. How is this person's life? Are they healthy? Are they happy?
What do they do? How do they get around?

When I do this exercise, I always smile. I imagine clean
energy, food, and water in abundance, social justice, and personalized medicine. I see cures for cancer and many other diseases.
I picture space travel as a regular part of life. Imagine groups of
friends planning moon excursions with the same flippant casu-
alness they would talk about going on a hike today. I envision
robots doing menial chores so people are free to create, connect,
and live full, happy lives. In short, I picture a significantly better
world than the one we live in today.

Whether your picture is the same as mine is not the point. If
there is any optimism in your vision, then we have to acknowledge that the path from today's world to a better future will
require an infusion of energy. I'd take it a step further and claim
that humans like you and me can create the future we want, but
we need a power source unrivaled in human history.

And that's where learning comes in. Instead of hoping for some
sort of abstract miracle, instead of waiting for other, more capable

people to solve problems, the transformational power to build the future lies within us. Specifically, it's the power of learning.

Do you believe that learning equals power? You might be tempted to dismiss the idea as trivial and obvious, but I would argue that most of us spend the majority of our waking hours in a state other than active, deliberate learning. We resist the learning process or avoid it altogether. If we really believed that learning equals power, then we would choose to learn much more often.

Making a conscious decision to learn, and reinforcing that decision frequently so that it becomes a mindset, is the first and most important step toward becoming an empowered learner. But it's not the only step. To be successful as a learner, it's important to expect setbacks and struggle and to embrace the fact that learning takes effort.

## Learning Is Work

We're born with an innate instinct for learning. It's the most natural thing in the world, but that doesn't make it easy. There's a video I love that illustrates this point. It shows a seven-month-old baby named Alice learning how to crawl. I saw it on Twitter, courtesy of Matt Bateman, who uses it to train Montessori teachers.

Watching baby Alice, it's easy to see she's hardwired to learn. Alice is lying on her tummy in the middle of a living room at the start of the video. She sees a bowl of toys across the rug and decides she wants one. She has never crawled before, but you can see in her face that she really wants to. She scrunches her legs, pushes with her feet, and throws out an arm in an attempt to propel herself forward. You can tell she's concentrating hard. She moves forward a bit and then falls and shouts and flops around. At one point, she rolls over onto her back. While this is happening, she's frequently looking at her mom behind the camera, who gives her constant positive messaging but never intervenes. In the end, Alice finally reaches the bowl. She grabs a cute wooden toy, and it goes right into her mouth. You want to cheer out loud!

Have you ever felt like this baby learning how to crawl? There are inevitable obstacles in your path. There is a painful gap between your current skill level and eventual success. You concentrate and work hard and exert yourself. Sometimes you move forward, and sometimes you fall back. Hopefully, there are people around you that care enough to cheer you on and support your learning, even if that means letting you struggle.

Learning is not for the faint of heart. It takes effort and persistence when it would be easy to quit. There are often more reasons not to learn a thing than to learn it, and the result is that real learning happens a lot less than it could.

## Why Don't We Learn?

Considering our innate instinct to be a learner and the rewarding feeling of satisfaction that comes from mastery, you might think we would all be empowered learners. And yet here we are reading a book about it. Why? What is getting in our way? Why don't we just learn all the time?

As it turns out, there are all sorts of barriers to learning. It's useful to point them out directly because you can notice them getting in your way. By recognizing them and understanding how they work, we can overcome these obstacles. I've grouped them into four main categories: biological, psychological, cultural, and human.

### BIOLOGICAL

There was a time when our early ancestors had very limited access to food and lived under constant threat of predators. Under these conditions, energy was scarce. Every day was a math equation with existential significance: do the calories coming in match the calories expended?

Now consider the disproportionate energy consumption of our brains. Even though your brain makes up just 2 percent of your mass, it can use 20–25 percent of the total energy of your body! So if you have the choice between calculating, processing, and inventing, or just following the group, which one will you pick? This is the reason we form tribes around sports teams, fashion brands, political parties, music groups, etc. It allows us to shut off the energy-intensive brain work.

Even more pressing than the threat of starvation: imagine you are in constant danger of attack from a predator or rival. You could hide in the cave with your group, or band together with your group to fight back. But you probably aren't going to tinker with some rock or bone you found lying around to invent a tool or weapon, even if that would make life better down the road. The reason? You are not safe! So instead of critical thinking, rational problem solving, and other forms of complex thought, your reptilian brain takes over with its familiar "fight or flight" mentality.

For many people in the world today, the human condition has changed. You are likely not facing scarcity of food and the threat of starvation. Hopefully, no one is trying to attack and kill you. But evolution is slow, and our brains today are still hardwired to respond to the dangers facing our earliest ancestors.

What does that mean? It means your brain is stuck in a mode of protecting you against dangers that are no longer there. You get tired of thinking and turn to Instagram or Netflix because your body is trying to conserve scarce glucose and ward off starvation. You have a visceral response to taking a risk or feeling stupid because your brain believes a predator might kill you.

These biological phenomena, while deeply rooted in our nature, are leading us in the exact opposite direction of being empowered learners.

## PSYCHOLOGICAL

Beyond evolutionary mechanisms and the conservation of brain energy, there are obstacles to learning that exist in our minds.

The best way to see this is to examine the scenario of giving a speech in public. The comedian Jerry Seinfeld once pointed out that the fear of public speaking shows up at the top of common lists of phobias, nudging out the fear of death. "This means that if you have to be at a funeral, you'd rather be in the casket than giving the eulogy!" It's funny because it's true: some experts estimate that 77% of people are afraid to speak in public. Why are so many of us terrified of standing in front of a group to speak?[3]

At the most basic level, we are afraid of failure. The feeling of trying and failing is such a blow to the ego, driving home messages about how unworthy and broken we are. If I try hard at this, and then I do a bad job, what does that mean about me? This inherent risk is present in public speaking and every other learning endeavor, and the result is anxiety and stress.

Like every other learning opportunity, speaking in public is a new and unfamiliar skill, and it's easy to feel like we don't measure up. The old-fashioned solution to this is to practice a lot, which is certainly helpful advice, but for many of us the fear never subsides. There's even a set of tools for mental health professionals focused on helping people through the fear of public speaking (the official term is glossophobia, if you're curious), which includes hypnotherapy visualization, mindfulness, and cognitive behavioral therapy.

Even more complicated, most of our learning activities happen in front of other people. In the public speaking example, we will be doing something new and scary in front of a crowd, and that adds additional layers of worry. We turn up the criticism knob, projecting onto our audience a level of scrutiny

---

[3] Lisa Fritscher, "Glossophobia or the Fear of Public Speaking," Verywell Mind, last updated July 16, 2021, https://www.verywellmind.com/glossophobia-2671860.

and negative judgment that crosses any sane boundary. What if people disagree with my ideas? What if there is something in my teeth? What if I wave my hands too much? What if my message is boring? What if they notice my eyes are different sizes?

There is one more layer of psychological barriers to learning. Let's imagine you are asked to speak at an event. You work hard to organize your thoughts and prepare your remarks. You practice in the mirror and with friends until you have the whole thing down pat. You do your breathing and visualization exercises and go on stage to speak. Now what are you thinking? This is where the fear and anxiety lead to imposter syndrome. Who am I to even be up here talking? I'm probably two seconds away from tanking! Does it seem like I think I'm smarter than everyone? These fears can create a strong pull down to the perceived average. After all, who wants to be accused of sitting on a high horse?

## CULTURAL

These types of worries cross from psychological to cultural obstacles. Similar to the fears we just talked about, we experience cultural barriers in our minds. But even though it happens in thoughts and feelings, cultural resistance to learning can be very real.

The education nonprofit Code.org made a video where Chris Bosh, the NBA basketball player, talks about an afterschool math program he did in high school, called the "Whiz Kids." His basketball friends would laugh and tease him about being into math, but he stuck with the program. He said, "I don't care, I'm learning a lot, and some of my friends have jobs."[4]

This story is typical, and it represents the kind of anti-learning sentiment present in many cultures. Have you heard terms like

---

[4] Code.org, "What Most Schools Don't Teach," February 26, 2013, YouTube video, 5:43, https://www.youtube.com/watch?v=nKIu9yen5nc.

brainiac, nerd, or teacher's pet? Too often, our broader cultural values discount or discourage learning.

Recent history is replete with examples of local subcultures pulling strongly against learning.

For example, Michael Oher spent his teenage years in and out of the foster care system, coming from a hard family background. He went to school because he had to, but the culture around him was hopeless and apathetic about learning. These are Michael's words from his 2011 memoir, *I Beat the Odds*:

> Mine [my teachers] pretty much didn't care if I was there or not…We would just be held in the classroom for the period and the teacher would go over the material, but nobody (including the teacher) seemed to care if it stuck or not. No one checked for homework or book reports or even gave many tests. When no one around you, at school or at home, seems to think learning is important, it's pretty hard to think that it is important yourself…[5]

Culture can go beyond apathy, crossing into direct opposition to learning. In his memoir, *Hillbilly Elegy*, J.D. Vance describes a strong pressure to stay with the group, even if that means skipping opportunities for learning and growth. He says, "Hillbillies have a phrase—'too big for your britches'— to describe those who think they're better than the stock they came from."[6] Unfortunately, this influence can be strong. Are you "too big for your britches" if you like to read? What about learning math and science? Speaking and writing with correct grammar? Is it culturally acceptable to set a goal or chase a big

---

[5] Michael Oher and Don Yaeger, *I Beat the Odds: From Homelessness to The Blind Side, and Beyond* (New York: Gotham Books, 2011), 82–83.

[6] J.D. Vance, *Hillbilly Elegy: A Memoir of a Family and Culture in Crisis* (London: William Collins, 2016), 30.

vision? It's hard enough to learn things, but if learning means facing open hostility from your friends and family, that's a much more challenging obstacle.

## HUMAN

Putting all of these factors together, you can see that becoming an empowered learner is an uphill climb. It's always easier, safer, and more comfortable to choose not to learn. And being human in the twenty-first century, there are plenty of things to do instead.

Right now, you are holding a paper book or a device while your eyes scan across symbols your brain turns into words with meaning. Then you have to gather those meanings and group them as ideas, turn them over in your mind, push back on them, and decide which ones you agree with. Maybe you're even applying the concepts to your own life, committing to be an empowered learner. It's a lot of effort!

While you are doing all of this hard work, there is likely a small rectangle just inches away, whispering seductively that all you have to do is tap a couple times and you can zone out in a video game, YouTube video, or Instagram reel. This is literally true: while writing this section about the distractions around us, I remembered I haven't done today's Wordle and took a break (I got it in two guesses!).

It's always easier and more fun to choose not to learn. Even when we are committed to being empowered learners, even when our learning is connected to our goals and dreams, even when we believe that the effort to learn will be worth it, the barrage of push notifications and the siren song of fine-tuned social algorithms are relentless.

Hopefully this section feels helpful and not overwhelming. Anytime you are trying to learn, there are a host of obstacles—biological, psychological, cultural, and human—that are standing in your way. But just because these challenges exist doesn't mean you are doomed to a life of complacency and pointlessness. You can become an empowered learner.

## How to Be an Empowered Learner

I know you're holding an entire book about it, but the path to becoming an empowered learner is actually just two simple steps: decide to learn, and learn how to learn.

### STEP ONE: DECIDE TO LEARN

It might seem obvious that the first step to learning (or doing anything else, for that matter) is to make a decision. There are entire shelves of books dedicated to setting an intention, manifesting into the universe, achieving your goals. Shia LaBeouf has a hilarious motivational speech about it: "DO IT!!"

But all jokes aside, there is literally no way to learn without first making the choice to do it. No one can trick you into learning, or get you to learn against your will. Learning is not a thing that happens to you. You have to make a decision to learn, and I'll argue that the more conscious you are of that decision-making process, the better off you'll be. This seemingly trivial concept actually runs in direct contrast to centuries of lived experience, where well-intentioned efforts to help other people learn resulted in an institutional forgetting that learning can only happen when a human makes a choice. As a result, most of us feel very little agency in the years between kindergarten and college graduation.

Unfortunately, the decision to learn is not a one-time affair. You can't simply "set it and forget it." Instead, powerful learning faces constant opposition. That means you might feel strongly about learning in one moment, and then the next day you find yourself bingeing Netflix episodes. Being an empowered learner requires a consistent choice.

## STEP TWO: LEARN HOW TO LEARN

Once you've decided to learn something, all you have to do is set about learning it. Simple, right? Not exactly.

Empowered learners see learning as their craft. They relentlessly practice the habits and routines that drive learning. They seek new methods and incorporate them, paying careful attention to the great learners around them and throughout history. They systematically identify and remove obstacles to their learning, whether structural or psychological. They ask questions, check sources, think out loud, and learn from mistakes.

In their book, *Talent*, Tyler Cowen and Daniel Gross ask would-be learners: "What is it you do to train that is comparable to a pianist practicing scales?"[7] The point is that learning takes focused effort, and the best learners consciously hone their craft.

When the subject matter is well-understood and clearly defined, such as swinging a golf club or performing music, being a great learner looks like deliberate practice: showing up for the reps, focusing with laser-like intensity on the learning frontier, and sticking with it for 10,000 hours.

But sometimes there is no textbook and the definition of success is nebulous, like in art or entrepreneurship or life. It's even more critical in these situations to know how to learn, because in addition to expanding knowledge and developing skills, the learner has to assess the goal itself.

Whether you are taking a course, practicing a musical instrument, or living your life, the surest path to meaning and success is being an empowered learner—making a conscious decision to learn, and getting really good at learning.

---

[7] Tyler Cowen and Daniel Gross, *Talent: How to Identify Energizers, Creatives, and Winners Around the World* (New York: St. Martin's Press, 2022).

## The Secret Recipe: Five Core Values

By this point in the book, you know what an empowered learner is, and you have the two big steps to become one: decide to learn, and learn how to learn. But you also have a sneaking suspicion that it's not so easy. You're right; it's not. The rest of this book is dedicated to the process of becoming an empowered learner. I hope you see yourself in all of this. I hope ideas will come to you about how you can apply these concepts for a more meaningful life, a life filled with contributions to others. Of course, the empowered learner concept is best when shared. So even though the main focus of this book is helping *you* become an empowered learner, we will pause along the way to explore these ideas in the context of helping others. At the end of each chapter, you'll find a short example of the principle in action, pulled from experiences I've had and people I've met while helping children become empowered learners.

As we embark on this journey together, I want to emphasize that the transformation I am inviting you to experience is inward and internal. You won't find a gold star sticker or ideal transcript or analytics dashboard that clearly proves that you are the best at learning. Becoming an empowered learner is a shift in mindset, a new way of seeing yourself and others in the world. Only you will really know it's happening. It's simultaneously audacious and vulnerable. It's also terrifying, for all the reasons we've already discussed.

I also want to be very clear that there is no magic checklist for becoming an empowered learner. There are no potions you can drink, no apps you can download, no forty-five-point plans. But there are basic truths—principles that, if understood and lived, will move you toward a life of meaning and contribution as an empowered learner.

These truths happen to be the five core values of Prenda, the company I founded to help people organize microschools. Taken together, these values represent the empowered learner way of thinking and being.

1. *Dare Greatly.* We discover our gifts and purpose, set big goals, then take small steps to achieve them. We hold ourselves to a high standard and we bravely continue when we hit a roadblock.

2. *Figure It Out.* We see ourselves as capable problem solvers who do whatever it takes to learn. We fearlessly question, we curiously tinker, and we stubbornly persist in our efforts to learn.

3. *Learning > Comfort* (pronounced "learning over comfort"). We choose to keep learning, even when it's hard. It may be tempting to avoid taking risks, but we know that meaningful learning and growth happen outside of our comfort zone.

4. *Start with Heart.* We see others as human beings with infinite value and unlimited potential. We reject labels and categories, focusing instead on humans who deserve empathy and inclusion.

5. *Foundation of Trust.* We generously extend trust to others and work hard to earn their trust in us. We assume good intentions and approach other people with empathy, curiosity, and compassion.

Do these sound like the empty, corporate core value statements that you write on a website and never think about again? I hope not, but maybe they do feel that way to you right now. Over the next five chapters, I hope to convince you that these values describe a better way of not only working, but living and learning too.

## CLIMBING A MOUNTAIN

For now, let's look at all five values together, lived out through the metaphor of hiking a mountain.

Imagine you are living your life, minding your own business, and you get the idea into your head to climb a mountain. Maybe it's a local peak that all your hiker friends do on weekends; maybe it's an expedition across continents to somewhere exotic and famous. You do some research, ask people about their experience, and one night you just decide: I am going to climb this mountain. You tell your loved ones about your intention, you write it down or post a photo of the destination on your bathroom mirror. You make a plan, arrange all the logistics, and when the appointed day arrives, you show up to the trailhead with your boots on, ready to start hiking. At this point, you are living the first value of an empowered learner, *Dare Greatly.*

You've done all kinds of internet research in your preparation, analyzing topological maps, choosing the trails that will lead you to the top. Now, as you begin your hike, you are watching for trail markers and rationing energy, food, and water. You may take a wrong turn, notice that what seemed like a trail was actually a dry waterway, and have to backtrack to resume your progress up the mountain. Perhaps you start to feel faint, and try to recover by resting in the shade and consuming a salty snack. As you solve the small and large problems you encounter along the trail, you are living the second value: *Figure It Out.*

So you're on your way! Assuming you can avoid freak accidents, scary wildlife, and abnormal weather, all you have to do is stay on the trail and keep moving forward. You'll eventually get there! Seems obvious, but it's not that easy. Hiking hurts. Your leg muscles will get tired. Your feet will hurt. Your heart and lungs will tire. As the day wears on, you are actively trading in the comfort of your non-hiking life for the thrill of something better.

The pain and blisters and sunburn and exhaustion are all part of the journey. You're adopting the value of *Learning > Comfort*.

What we've mentioned so far would be enough to get you to the top of the mountain, except for one important thing: you're not hiking alone! You are with a group of friends who have chosen the same goal, and together you are working your way up the trail. Being with a group adds a layer of comfort, safety, and fun to the experience. You're glad they came, but doing something with other humans also introduces complexity. What if one member of your group has an injury or mental breakdown? What if you don't agree about the right direction to go? Over the course of the hike, there will be moments where the other people with you will be a great support, and other moments where they are a burden. With the value of *Start with Heart*, you choose to see other humans in a respectful, positive way, embracing the truth of the proverb: if you want to go fast, go alone; if you want to go far, go together.

As you recognize the value of hiking in a group and choose to see others as humans, you come to rely on your fellow hikers. You believe that they will help you if you need it, and they believe the same thing about you. We call this a *Foundation of Trust*, recognizing that an implicit measure of trust is at the core of every human interaction. With high trust among our groups, we can collaborate, build, solve, learn, and accomplish in ways that none of us could do alone. Actively building trust with others turns learning from a solo act to a team sport, unlocking benefits that far outweigh the sum of the parts.

Putting these behaviors together, you are well on your way to the summit of your mountain. You have all the ingredients for accomplishing a goal that matters to you, becoming the person you want to be, and making a difference for others as well.

## Empowered Learners in Action

But learning is not limited to grandiose adventures; after all, hiking the mountain is just a metaphor. You can apply the five core values to be an empowered learner in every aspect of your life, big or small.

Recently, I was helping my wife with some home improvement. In one of the bedrooms, we noticed that the electrical outlet was old, discolored and spattered with paint drops; it didn't match the freshly painted trim. This room would look nicer if this outlet was replaced. Could I do it? Since I had never done any electrical work before, the whole thing felt a little scary.

So I did what any empowered learner would do—went to YouTube and watched videos of experts showing how to replace an outlet. "Not so bad," I thought. Let's *Dare Greatly*. First step: *Figure It Out*. Between the videos and a step-by-step article I found online, I learned to shut off the power to that bedroom, remove the wall plate, unscrew the old outlet, and disconnect the wires that connected it to the electrical wiring of the house. Pausing and replaying the YouTube video, I was frustrated to find that my situation did not exactly match what I was seeing on screen. One of the wires was a different color: new internet search. One of the screws that came with the new outlet was too short: trip to the hardware store to get a longer one. It was *Learning > Comfort*, but eventually I got the new outlet installed, turned on the power, and plugged in a light to show off my accomplishment to my wife and kids. With some new confidence in myself and elevated trust from my wife, I moved on to install a light switch and then a ceiling fan. No electrocutions yet, knock on wood.

This same learning loop is available to anyone in every topic. Changing the brakes on your car, mastering a Beethoven sonata on piano, getting an ordinance passed in City Council, building a center to aid refugees, finishing a graduate degree, launching an entrepreneurial venture. The possibilities are endless.

Learning looks different in every situation and for every person, but if you look closely you can see these same concepts applied.

I was surprised when my son Bennett came home from school and mentioned that he'd signed up for a Kenpo karate class. None of us had any experience with martial arts and I had no idea he was interested. I remember him coming home from that first lesson with a paper full of terms. It was such a long list, all in small print, with crazy names like "Deflecting Hammer" and "Sword of Destruction." He didn't know anything! But gradually, day by day, he showed up to practice, watched demonstrations, and worked slowly through the movements. He learned the basic salute and routine for entering and exiting the mat. I saw him reciting moves in his head, silently moving through the stances and movements of the various forms, sets, and techniques. He asked me to quiz him, reading a move from the list for him to demonstrate. He signed up for class after class and kept practicing at home. At first, his movements were awkward as he thought about each step in the sequence. Over time, he looked more natural. In an assembly at the end of the school year, he and another student simulated an entire fight scene filled with kicks and punches, blocks and throws. I was astonished watching him demonstrate mastery of the martial art in his black belt test.

One day, a neighbor knocked on our door and handed my son Asher an old acoustic guitar. Asher immediately started experimenting with it, quickly learning the four chords I taught him and then surpassing me with the help of YouTube tutorials. His fingers formed calluses after hours of choosing *Learning > Comfort*. As he improved, he found himself collaborating with others to write songs and perform them. He found that music works best when you *Start with Heart*.

The five core values show up in formal, academic learning too. When I was a graduate student, I signed up for a course called Plasma Transport Physics, where we tried to describe the movement of charged particles in a magnetic field using math that I had never seen before. I struggled through the semester, hitting a low point about six weeks in when my instructor called me into his office to say my performance wasn't cutting it. With patient support from Professor Peter Catto, help from my classmates, and many hours of *Figure It Out* and *Learning > Comfort*, I was able to pass the class.

You don't have to be enrolled in school to be an empowered learner. My father-in-law, John Schroeder, is a great example. He learned the plumbing trade fifty years ago, first as an apprentice and then as a plumber of increasing skill. He recently sold the plumbing business he ran for the last decade. I've watched him on the job. It's miraculous. He will walk into a home that has a leak, listen quietly to the homeowner, and then start a gauntlet of science experiments to *Figure It Out*. He'll turn on the cold water, shut off the hot, and feel the flow in a particular pipe. He drives sound waves through a pipe and detects vibrations on the other end. Sometimes his process relies on sophisticated technology; other times it is a trick master plumbers have used for generations.

When I'm "assisting" John, I end up asking a barrage of questions, trying to access the underlying systems diagrams and the corresponding logic tree that exists in his mind after decades of solving these types of problems. Even more impressive is his ability to optimize for things like destruction of the house; he is often called in by the insurance company after other plumbers needlessly dig up the floors, poke holes in walls, and tear out cabinets. John applies his learning to do great work with minimal impact, *Daring Greatly* to avoid the waste of mistakes, which means he does better work *and* costs less than your average plumber. My father-in-law doesn't have a college degree, but he's one of the best learners I have ever seen.

## What About School?

By now, I hope the concept of an empowered learner is resonating with you. I genuinely believe you and everyone around you will be better off as you make learning your quest. But you may be a bit skeptical, or at least complacent. After all, don't we already have a society focused on learning? What about this framed piece of paper hanging on the wall of my office? Isn't the institution of school already set up for this exact purpose?

Up to this point in the book, we haven't talked about formal education. I'll say right off the bat that I am a huge proponent of the ideas behind our current systems—learning as a means of advancing yourself and society, sharing resources so that opportunity is open to everyone. But I will also claim that the structures and subcultures of the traditional classroom often misalign with the goal of empowering learners. Sometimes, children become empowered learners at school, but that is not the norm. And too often, the experience in the classroom has the exact opposite effect, leading to the second equation:

$$School \neq Learning$$

My personal story is a prime example. I was one of those kids for whom school came easy. I had a knack for memorizing facts, so I did well on multiple choice tests. I was good at following algorithms, so I got good scores on the papers I wrote with the cynical aim of giving the teachers what they wanted. I studied the syllabus, figured out the rules, and made a game out of doing the minimum amount of effort to still get an A in the class. I bragged to friends that all of my grades were between 90 and 91 percent, meaning I did not do an ounce of work beyond what was required.

I graduated salutatorian in my high school class with all As and a scholarship to college. At the time, I considered this a success. After all, I had entered a playing field with 900 peers and finished in second place. My educator grandparents were definitely enthusiastic. But was my experience an example to be replicated?

Maybe not, according to Karen Arnold, a professor and researcher in the Education School at Boston College. Karen and her team tracked a set of eighty-one valedictorians and salutatorians from their conspicuous success in high school throughout their life. She was not surprised to see this group of achievers do well in college and get high-paying jobs, but she also noticed that they were "not likely to be the future's visionaries...they typically settle into the system instead of shaking it up."[8]

Now let's take a look at another personal story, this time from my mom. Growing up in the 1960s, my mom and her sisters were unique in that they received strong encouragement to pursue an education. My mother approached her schoolwork with gusto, doing well as a child and developing a love of reading and a talent for writing. But when she was eight years old, she had a math teacher who emphasized the speed of math facts, having the children face off with multiplication problems in front of the class, and then seating them in the order of the competition. Sort of a math *Hunger Games*. My mom hadn't memorized the times table yet and she did not thrive in the public, speedy, and competitive environment. She ended up in the last place seat and stayed there through the semester. She started believing a lie—that her brain was not wired for math, that she would never be able to get it. She sat quietly in the back, hoping no one would discover her secret—that she didn't understand. This compounded over the following years. Her eighth grade teacher showed visible annoyance with her attempts to learn, dismissed her as a lost cause he just wanted to pass along to the

[8] Adam Grant, "What Straight-A Students Get Wrong," opinion, *New York Times*, December 8, 2018, https://www.nytimes.com/2018/12/08/opinion/college-gpa-career-success.html.

next teacher, and told her, "Just copy down my solutions." After years of bad test scores and negative experiences with math, my mom walked away with a psychological block that made high school and college a major challenge. Decades later, as she was fulfilling a lifelong goal of finishing her undergraduate degree, she still had to fight through the shadow of these early experiences in math.

In both my story and my mom's, you can see behaviors that run counter to the ideals of an empowered learner. We picked up these habits in rational response to the structure and system we were presented with.

I'd argue that most people do the same thing. Some think, *Tell me what I have to do and I'll meet your requirements with the minimum amount of effort.* Others think, *I'm broken or deficient anyway, so what's the use in trying?* These attitudes are not learning, at least not the aspirational, exciting, powerful kind of learning we are talking about in this book.

If you believe me that school, as we know it today, does not equal learning, then you might be wondering why. *How did we get here? What is school all about if not learning? Is there a better way?* I need to say unequivocally that the challenges in traditional education are not the result of unintelligent or immoral people. On the contrary, our education system is full of some of the best folks you can find, brimming with altruism and a commitment to the important work at hand. Classroom teachers, in particular, are faced with a tough job that continues to get harder, while pay falls short and respect may even be on a decline. By and large, these people show up with great competence and care, and for that we should all be grateful.

But if you ask classroom teachers, you will find that there is a real problem. The list of job requirements gets longer each legislative session. The regulatory regime around standardized testing presents an obstacle to real learning. Kids are coming to school with trauma and a variety of life challenges that the structure is not built to support. Is the system as we know it empowering learners?

Too often, children in traditional classrooms decide to keep their unique gifts hidden and undiscovered. Fear of getting the wrong answer prevents them from exploring their exciting potential. Many children never have a caring adult that sees and understands what they are capable of. Even for the lucky ones with supportive adults in their lives, the implied message is: "Sit in this chair, do the things we ask, and in thirteen years you will be ready for a successful, happy life."

It's simply not true. The reason is foundational; the underlying philosophy of a system that transmits information is incompatible with the real goal of empowering learners. Remember the Plutarch quote? "The mind is not a vessel to be filled, but a fire to be kindled." With the best of intentions and the best of people, traditional education was designed to fill vessels. Picture a growing list of curriculum standards, a Pavlovian set of penalties and rewards, high-stakes testing, and a pedagogy that has been slow to evolve from "sage on the stage."

Reid Hoffman and Ben Casnocha describe the same phenomenon in their book, *The Startup of You*. Focusing on the part of life after high school graduation, they employ the metaphor of an escalator. We believe that if we get on the right escalator through a college degree, a job, the right credentials, etc., then the escalator will take us to our destination. The problem with this strategy, according to Hoffman and Casnocha? The escalator is jammed. In other words, life is not a passive ride through the institutions and structures controlled by others. Instead, you set the course, you make the plans, and you do the work. It's more of an entrepreneurial adventure than an escalator ride.

Instead of filling vessels, imagine an education system designed to kindle a fire in the minds of young people. It would require a deep commitment to the mission of empowering learners and a constant emphasis on the core values we just discussed. But promoting correct principles is not enough; the structure itself needs a fresh look.

There is a lot more we could say about the structure of the education system, but that is the subject for another book. For now, I invite you to consider how your life and the lives of your loved ones would be different if you were an empowered learner.

## The "Empowered Learner" Way

There was a day during my first semester of running a microschool when I was not feeling well. I could barely get out of bed. Because we were small and scrappy and meeting at my house, I had a bit of a dilemma. What am I going to do? In desperation, I called one of the moms, who agreed to be the adult chaperone. She didn't have a lot of experience with the learning approach, other than hearing her kids talk about how much they loved school, and her confidence was shaky because she was relatively new to the United States and was still learning English. I assured her that the kids knew what to do, and then prayed silently from my bedroom down the hall as I heard the group kick off the morning routine.

At one point in the day, I lay in bed staring up at the ceiling, barely conscious and a little bit sweaty, listening to the class through the closed door. They were engaging in a Socratic discussion, led by one of the kids, about whether robots will take over all of our jobs.

I rolled over in bed and strained my ear to hear a little more. I could hear each of the students sharing thoughts and observations from an article they had read in advance. They referenced notes they had taken. They asked open-ended questions and responded to each other, building on insights and having a fantastic conversation. I heard widely varying opinions and a healthy back and forth, with civility that exceeds your average Twitter feed. All the kids were engaged and participating, and I never once heard the voice of the adult chaperone.

At this moment, I realized that something special was happening. It was a moment of pure, unadulterated, empowering learning. I knew that I had to do everything in my power to bring this type of learning to as many people as possible. That's why I started Prenda, and that's why I'm writing this book.

Empowered learners believe different things and behave in different ways than the average person. They push aside fears to set big goals. They worry less about what other people think and instead operate from a clear sense of identity and purpose. They take ownership of their learning and their life, as opposed to waiting for external permission. They persevere through hard times instead of giving up. They are abundant and generous with others, rather than feeling threatened and acting petty. They believe in themselves and others in a way that seems almost scary.

I believe empowered learners live more meaningful lives. I believe empowered learners will move humanity forward. I believe you can be an empowered learner. Are you ready?

# Empowered Learner Vignette:

# Mollie's Story

THE ARIZONA SUN WAS SHINING BRIGHT AS MY WIFE, KIMBERLY, stepped out of the air-conditioned car and walked across the asphalt parking lot. Passing the marquis sign and the flagpole, she opened the door of the school office and registered as a visitor. It was the first parent–teacher conference of the year, and she was meeting with the first grade teacher of our daughter, Mollie.

For fifteen straight minutes, the teacher raved about Mollie, praising her stellar attitude and diligence in her schoolwork. Kim looked over the progress report, a long list of the things the school expects of first graders, and corresponding letters next to each of them. There were a couple areas of possible improvement, but the overall picture was that of a model student. Later that night, we beamed with pride as we reflected on Mollie's success.

But everything changed a few weeks later when Kim was volunteering in Mollie's classroom. While she helped prepare some phonics packets from the back of the room, she watched Mollie, and noticed something alarming: this wasn't our daughter!

At home, Mollie's feisty personality was on display. Funny, clever, always moving, always curious, social, friendly, competitive, and fully committed when she set her mind to a goal. Watching her in that first grade classroom, Kim saw a girl who was afraid, rigid, disengaged, formal, compliant, placating the adults, waiting for the day to end. It was like she was playing a part, denying her true gifts and personality to "go with the program." She didn't make a peep. No wonder the teacher liked her so much!

I didn't have the words for it at the time, but what my wife saw in our daughter is the exact opposite of an empowered learner. She wouldn't ask a question because she didn't want to disrupt the class. She didn't get excited about projects, just obediently finished all her assignments. As the fire gradually went out, Mollie experienced the same thing as millions of students—disengagement. According to a recent Gallup poll, 75 percent of fifth graders report being engaged at school. This number drops to 34 percent for high school seniors. Trends like this feel troubling, but it was startling to see it firsthand in our precious daughter.

The next year, as I started working on the microschool concept that would become Prenda and piloted a microschool around our kitchen table, these moments came back to mind. Every day, I watched seven kids take ownership of their education. They stood face-to-face each morning to declare their intentions and announce their goals for a feeling of mutual accountability. They dove into "conquer mode," where they worked at their learning frontier to master core academic subjects like language and math. During "collaborate mode," they worked as a group on exciting science projects, explored the great moments of history, and debated current events. They teamed up in pairs during "create mode," inventing taxonomy of species for a fictional planet, designing protective apparatuses for an egg drop competition, and performing original TED Talks.

Pedagogy experts would see the model and talk about blended learning, personalization, mastery, inquiry, and project-based learning. But for the seven kids in my microschool, it was *fun*. They felt themselves becoming learners.

Mollie noticed this too, and pretty soon she was begging me to let her join a microschool. We finished the pilot semester, and the next year I opened a microschool for Mollie and her friends. Before long, Kim and I could see the fire kindling in Mollie's eyes. She got competitive and fierce, taking on stretch goals. Her playful wit and curiosity shone through her projects. And her fun and friendly demeanor lit up the room. Our girl was back.

# Chapter 2

# Dare Greatly

—

DO YOU EVER THINK YOUR LIFE IS HARD? WHEN I CATCH MYSELF setting up the decorations for a personal pity party, I try to remember that other people have faced challenges that make my problems look silly in comparison. Some of those people overcame challenges and made remarkable contributions to the world around them. Take Frederick Douglass, for example.

Born to an enslaved mother and separated as an infant, Frederick's entire childhood was defined by loss, isolation, and brutal oppression. At age six, he was taken from his grandmother to work on a plantation. He was treated as property, "gifted," transferred, and put to work as a slave. He was brutally beaten and frequently whipped on top of the grueling physical labor he was forced to do, day in and day out.

Fortunately for Frederick and every human on the planet, he saw the inherent injustice in his situation and persistently refused to allow slavery to hold him back. He picked up a rudimentary understanding of the alphabet from a kind neighbor. He taught himself to read and write, using the only book he could get his hands on—the Bible. He escaped slavery after multiple failed attempts, sneaking through Delaware and finding his way to a famous abolitionist in New York. He courted Anna Murray from several states away, marrying her and raising five children together. He literally changed his name and embarked on a fresh start as a free man.

One thing I love about Frederick Douglass is his uncontainable desire to help other people. While it would have been easy to choose a relaxing lifestyle in quiet anonymity after his escape, Frederick instead devoted his life to lifting others, ending slavery, and supporting good causes. Even before his escape from the plantation, he was teaching other enslaved people to read and write. After escaping, he launched a newsletter, wrote two autobiographies, and gave public speeches about his experiences. Frederick's words shone a bright light on the immorality of slavery, changing public opinion and driving toward emancipation.

Later in life, Frederick Douglass called out Abraham Lincoln, drove three amendments to the US Constitution, served as an ambassador for the country, received presidential ballot votes, and expanded his reach to support women's suffrage and other causes.

Throughout his entire life, Frederick faced opposition and hostility from people who disagreed with him. He was physically assaulted. He was defamed and mocked. He was dismissed in the most inhumane ways. Even people friendly to his cause made limiting assumptions about Frederick based on the color of his skin.

What drove Frederick Douglass? Where did he find the tenacity to break out of literal oppression and bondage and embark on a new life? Why did he accept the ongoing struggle and opposition that comes with trying to make a difference in the world?

Part of the mystery lies deep within. Frederick believed something powerful about himself, and that core belief transcended his immediate circumstances, the beliefs of others, and even the law of probability.

This is how he described his core belief:

From my earliest recollection, I date the entertainment of a deep conviction that slavery would not always be able to hold me within its foul embrace; and in the darkest hours of my career in slavery, this living word of faith and spirit of hope departed not from me, but remained like ministering angels to cheer me through the gloom.[9]

Frederick was born enslaved, mistreated all his life, and deprived of basic human rights and dignity. But he didn't see those evils as defining or limiting. He knew he was more than his situation. He had lofty ambitions. He worked long and hard, and his efforts served not only himself and his family but enslaved and oppressed people everywhere, leaving the entire world better than he found it.

Frederick Douglass embodies the value of Dare Greatly. Understanding his unique gifts, he set out to tackle one goal after another.

One frame that can help make sense of the story of Frederick Douglass, and countless other people who have made a positive impact, is the Hero's Journey. This is the classic tale of a protagonist, pulled from the ordinary world to face challenges, accumulate experiential growth, and emerge as a better person. Even if you don't recognize the Hero's Journey by name, you probably know the basic storyline by heart. It plays out over and over again in our folklore, whether in Greek mythology, Disney cartoons, or Tolkien novels. It's the story of a young prince named Siddhartha Gautama, who left his comfortable palace home on a quest for understanding, and became the enlightened Buddha.

Malala Yousafzai responded to an inner call to speak up for girls' right to an education. Barack Obama stepped into the limelight after realizing he could make a difference. But you

---

[9] Frederick Douglass, *Narrative of the Life of Frederick Douglass, an American Slave* (North Carolina: Academic Affairs Library, UNC-CH, University of North Carolina at Chapel Hill, 1999), electronic edition, https://docsouth.unc.edu/neh/douglass/douglass.html.

don't have to be famous to experience the Hero's Journey; it shows up in the lives of regular people shaping our world today.

In her book, *Courage to Grow*, Laura Sandefer describes how she and her husband Jeff have built an entire school concept, called the Acton Academy, on the premise that each human being is on a Hero's Journey. From her very first newspaper advertisement, Laura invited children and their families into the Hero's Journey. Each child to walk into an Acton Academy becomes the hero of their very own adventure story.

It's one thing to respond to a call, to have a big idea, or to feel inspired to live life on a different plane. Most of us have whims and wishes. The challenge is to make it real: turning your idea into a clear goal that you understand and believe in, then taking the first steps toward achieving it. This is what we mean by the value of Dare Greatly.

If you're a fan of Theodore Roosevelt, you may recognize the phrase "Dare Greatly." It comes from a speech he gave in Paris, a year after leaving office as President of the United States. These words have become a rallying cry for those who choose to live their life "in the arena," as opposed to criticizing from the sidelines.

> It is not the critic who counts; not the man who points out how the strong man stumbles or where the doer of deeds could have done them better. The credit belongs to the man who is actually in the arena, whose face is marred by dust and sweat and blood…who at the best knows in the end the triumph of high achievement, and who at the worst, if he fails, at least fails while **daring greatly** [emphasis mine], so that his place shall never be with those cold and timid souls who neither know victory nor defeat.[10]

---

[10] Theodore Roosevelt, "Address at the Sorbonne in Paris, France: 'Citizenship in a Republic,' April 23, 1910," The American Presidency Project, accessed February 6, 2023, https://www.presidency.ucsb.edu/documents/address-the-sorbonne-paris-france-citizenship-republic.

In her book, *Daring Greatly*, researcher and media personality Brené Brown provides a modern interpretation of this empowering approach to life, focusing less on the literal sweat and dust and blood that would have accompanied Teddy Roosevelt on a safari or battlefield, and instead on the choice to live wholeheartedly, courageously, and vulnerably, pursuing our dreams without fearing the negative opinions of others.

The entrance gate to the arena floor is wide open and everyone is invited. You don't have to be a special breed of human. There is no checklist of requirements to be allowed to live life in this way, no government agency begrudgingly handing out licenses. As you'll find out in this chapter, daring greatly is really just two simple steps: choosing a mountain, and climbing it.

But an overwhelming majority of people spend their entire lives without ever daring greatly. Why not? What is stopping them? What is stopping you?

## Step 1: Choose a Mountain

The first step to daring greatly is to pick a goal. There are entire books dedicated to goal-setting, so I won't try to lay out the full theory here. My favorite argument for the wisdom of setting a goal is expressed by the Cheshire Cat in the Disney cartoon version of *Alice in Wonderland*. Alice finds herself at a crossroads in a dark forest, with signs pointing in all directions. She encounters a talking cat. You might remember the sequence:

> *Alice: I wanted to ask you which way I ought to go.*
> *Cheshire Cat: That depends on where you want to get to.*
> *Alice: Oh, it really doesn't matter...*
> *Cheshire Cat: Then it really doesn't matter which way you go.*[11]

---

[11] *Alice in Wonderland*, directed by Clyde Geronimi, Wilfred Jackson, and Hamilton Luske (1951; Burbank, CA: Walt Disney Productions).

Daring greatly is the deliberate act of envisioning a future state and committing yourself to making it real. If you've tried this before, you know that it's harder than it sounds. But hopefully you've also enjoyed the feeling of accomplishing a goal.

One way to think about daring greatly is the analogy of hiking up a mountain. It is always easier and more comfortable to stay home, but there is a reason 57 million people in the US choose to go hiking. There is something within us that longs for the challenge, yearns for the feeling of overcoming, and anticipates the glory of arriving at the top.

To Dare Greatly is to apply this hiker's mindset to anything you want to do in life. The first step is choosing a mountain to climb. Fortunately, there is no shortage of options.

MOUNTAINS ALL AROUND

In physics and engineering, there is a concept called "local maxima," where a particular math problem might have several points that stand out as higher than everything around them. It is kind of like a mountain range, where there are multiple solutions to a given problem, and the "right" one depends on the starting point and the specific application. This chart of a made-up math function illustrates the concept:

The main thing to notice from this picture is that there are many peaks. They vary in shape and size, and there is no sign pointing to the correct peak. This is true for your life. The challenge is not to climb the same mountain as everyone around you, but to choose the mountain that lights a fire for you. If you look around, ask lots of questions, and try new things, you will realize that the world is full of mountains to climb. Some are tall, some are short. Some are steep, some more gradual.

To Dare Greatly, we must recognize that there are many mountains to climb and choose one. This requires that we first reject the idea of a single mountain that all of us must climb. Our post-industrial world has done us a disservice on this front, implying that there is a one-dimensional path to success, as if we were Model T cars on a Henry Ford assembly line. Standardized tests, college admissions, and rigidly defined career tracks all reinforce the idea of a single mountain for everyone, instead of the (much more interesting) reality that there are mountains all around us, waiting to be climbed.

## These are all local maxima

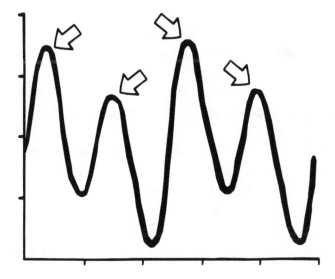

KNOW THYSELF

Once you can see that there are mountains all around, you are ready to choose one to start climbing. This is a personal decision, so it will depend heavily on who you are as a person. Choosing the right mountain for you will be easier if you follow the ancient Greek wisdom to "know thyself."

Have you ever come to a crossroads where you feel like there are multiple mountains you could choose to climb? Maybe you are interested in several of them, and choosing one feels like permanently shutting off the others.

I had this happen when I arrived at college and the admissions people asked me to declare a major. I was so excited for college. The ability to choose my courses and have more input in my learning journey was very appealing to me, and I immediately began exploring the different departments on campus. I was naturally good at math, so maybe a math or statistics major? I love reading, writing, and ideas, so maybe I should choose something in the humanities? I've always had a practical bent, so maybe something like engineering or business where I could get a job afterward? After talking it over with my wise father (who had seven different college majors himself), I decided on physics. It was something I genuinely loved learning about, and it seemed to keep many options open in case I changed my mind in the future.

There are all kinds of questions you could ask in the process of knowing thyself. What am I good at? What comes easily to me? Where would my effort pay off? These are all relevant, but they neglect the concept of purpose.

Martin Luther King Jr. grew up around the ministry. His father preached sermons for forty years at the Ebenezer Baptist Church in Atlanta, and much of the family life and community involvement at the King home revolved around church. So it was not surprising that young Martin decided to attend seminary on the path to being a minister himself.

But even as he was developing his voice and style giving sermons, Martin felt a pull to the secular and found himself drawn to the Civil Rights movement. He met with Howard Thurman, the American Civil Rights leader, who told him: "Don't ask what the world needs. Ask what makes you come alive, and go do that, because what the world needs are people who have come alive."

What makes you come alive? One way to find out if a particular mountain is the right one for you to climb is to get as close as you can to it and see how it feels. Are you doing the obligatory reading, or are you voraciously devouring everything you can find on the topic? Are you "padding your resume," or are you taking every opportunity to get close to the work, meeting the people, and showing up for the events? If you didn't need money, would you still be spending time on this?

In the book *Dark Horse*, researchers Todd Rose and Ogi Ogas document case after case of people who left a traditional or established path to seek personal fulfillment. Beneath all of these stories, a commitment to "know thyself" gave people the courage to step away from the one-dimensional "success formula" and find a mountain that suited them better.

## SET THE ALTITUDE

Have you ever heard the expression "flying too close to the sun"? It comes from the story of Icarus in Greek mythology.

As the story goes, Icarus and his father, Daedalus, are trapped in a labyrinth on the island of Crete. There are too many twists and turns and they're unable to get out of the maze. Daedalus, an Athenian craftsman, engineers wings from feathers and wax for an aerial escape.

You might remember the tragic ending of the story. Despite his father's warning to avoid flying too high, Icarus is so enthralled with his ability to fly that he goes too close to the sun, where his wings melt away, leading to his horrifying death.

The moral of the story is the exact opposite of Dare Greatly. Disguised behind well-intentioned concern and the logical advice to avoid hubris, we hear in this story the familiar refrain that we can't do it, that it's dangerous to try. Hence the conventional wisdom and limiting self-talk. "Play it safe." "Stay in your lane." "Don't rock the boat."

But is that really always the best approach?

Seth Godin shares the forgotten part of the story in his book, *Icarus Deception: How High Will You Fly.* Before taking off on their escape from the labyrinth, Daedalus actually gives his son two warnings. Yes, he cautions against hubris and flying too high with a bad physics lesson (it actually isn't hotter at high altitudes, unless you get to the ionosphere, but then you have different problems). But he also warns his son against complacency, explaining that flying too low will lead to heavy, wet wings from the ocean mists. Both problems—flying too high and flying too low—lead to a crash landing.

It's important to consider both lessons from Icarus when choosing a goal. The best goals are attainable, in accordance with the laws of physics, reasonable preparation, and basic logic. For me, flying too high might be a goal in playing professional basketball (physical limitations) or performing brain surgery (practical realities). But the best goals also stretch us to be something more. And because we are much more likely to set goals that are too low than too high, it makes sense to ask ourselves: in what ways am I limiting myself before I even get started? The goal to finish a season of a show on Netflix might be fun, but it doesn't inspire.

## SEE IT IN YOUR MIND

Instead of talking yourself out of climbing a mountain, you can "try on" success by visualizing yourself taking that path and making it to the top. Ask yourself these questions:

- What does a typical day look like if I pursue this goal?

- How will I know I have been successful?

- What does that feel like?

- Who are the people I will associate with on this journey?

- Do I care about their opinion of me? Why or why not?

- What can I do from the top of this mountain that I can't do now?

- How do I feel about doing that work long after everyone stops noticing?

Throughout the process of seeing a vision, it's critical to make sure it's what you really want, and not what others say you should want. A fictional anecdote by Heinrich Boll illustrates this point with some biting humor, when an ambitious businessman meets a local fisherman and launches into a diatribe about how working harder would lead to more money, a bigger operation, and eventually a big payout so he could live a restful life at the beach—the exact life the man already had!

One perpetual challenge with the process of visualizing a potential path is getting good information. How can you get an accurate picture of what this road would be like? Think of all the medical students who are years into a program before discovering they can't stand the sight of blood. Or the casual video gamers who have no idea about the focused practice hours put in by eSports competitors. To reduce the risk of disappointment later, I recommend talking to as many people as you can find. Ask them sincere questions about their life on the path you are exploring. What are their favorite and least favorite moments? What do they do every day? See if they will let you follow them around and watch, or even help with some of their work.

Collecting this type of real-life information about the mountains around you will help you know which might be a good fit.

## MAKE A COMMITMENT

At this point, you recognize that there are many mountains you could climb, you've thought about what makes you come alive, you've checked to make sure the mountain isn't too small or too high, and you've visualized yourself on top. What now?

The first thing to do is breathe. These moments can feel scary and permanent, like you're committing to a one-way road for the rest of your life. Having lived through many of these moments, I can tell you that there will be plenty of chances to evaluate, and plenty of time to try other things. Our brains are wired to avoid FOMO (fear of missing out), but it just doesn't serve us here. So take a deep breath, and let's go!

Choosing a mountain doesn't have to be a one-time, high-stakes decision. Most successful people I know have experimented with a variety of things before committing to their current mountain. My friend Rajiv fell in love with the guitar as a twelve-year-old. He got a job washing dishes at a local restaurant, saved up the money, and bought his first guitar. From that point, he just played relentlessly, ending up on tour with some older musicians when he was just sixteen. Rajiv learned a lot from those exciting days as a rock star, which he later applied to his successful career in sales and his current business, a chain of old-timey barber shops that are so popular it can take weeks to get an appointment.

The secret is not to pick the single mountain you will climb for the rest of your life. Instead, look around at your current options and pick the best one available to you right now. Do you have a mountain in mind? Ready for the next step?

## Step 2: Start Climbing

Once you identify a big goal that catches your interest and feels just the right amount intimidating, it's time to start climbing. If you don't have a mountain in mind yet, don't worry! Just continue the thoughtful reflection of the first step, looking around, asking questions, and seeking. My only caution here is that you might be over-analyzing. Better to start climbing a mountain you're unsure about than to not start at all.

Take me, for example. When I was in eighth grade, my teacher brought in materials about a variety of college majors and career paths. I read everything, took the quiz, and decided that journalism was the path for me. I dreamed in a very abstract way about a future life as a reporter. Flipping through the brochures and reference books (this was pre-internet), I found that the University of Nebraska at Lincoln had a strong journalism department, and I decided that was the place for me. I did the first half of Daring Greatly, choosing the mountain of journalism, and then I stopped. My eighth-grade self didn't realize I could do anything more. Needless to say, I did not become a journalist.

If I was advising my younger self today, I would tell that kid to get busy climbing the mountain. Find a compelling topic and write about it. Launch a blog on Medium or a newsletter on Substack. Tell a story no one else is telling, even if you're the only one who cares about it. Research inspiring reporters and email them out of the blue. Start a school newspaper. Many of these options were available to me. Heaven knows I had plenty of time in the day. No one was stopping me or discouraging me. I just didn't know I was "allowed" to start climbing the mountain.

The poet William Wordsworth understood this simple but powerful idea more than 200 years ago. He said simply, "To begin, begin."

## ONE STEP AT A TIME

The best advice I can give you is to start climbing. Find one small thing that would take you in the direction of your goal, then find another. It doesn't matter that you can't see the entire path in detail; things will make sense as you learn more. For now, the goal is to learn by doing. Your small step could be anything:

- Read articles or books on the topic.

- Watch video interviews of an expert.

- Email the expert with questions.

- Meet in person with someone involved in the work.

- Try the activity at a small scale.

- Attend gatherings of a community built around your interest.

- Sign up for a course, tutoring, or private lessons.

- Write about your interest and post your work.

- Start a podcast and interview people you find interesting.

You might feel uncomfortable about some of these steps; they certainly can feel like "putting yourself out there." We'll talk about that in Chapter 4: Learning > Comfort. The other thing you might notice is that these activities typically don't cost a lot of money, and they usually don't involve a financial payout. There are exceptions, of course, but for the most part you can learn in ways that cost very little out of pocket. So as long as you are willing and able to forgo the income you might be making with your time in a less learning-intensive pursuit, then Daring Greatly is available to you. If you are young, with no pressure to provide for yourself (e.g., a teenager living at home), then solving for the financial part of the equation is easy. If you have mouths to feed, you can still Dare Greatly, but it may require moonlighting, spending time outside your nine-to-five job.

One of the best examples of Daring Greatly is my friend David Perell. Like many young, smart people, David felt like he had something to say. He read posts from folks all over the internet and set a goal to be a writer. Unlike most people his age, David didn't see a writing career as something to be handed to him by some gatekeeper. Instead, he committed to writing every day, and he just got better and better. Today his work reaches millions of people, through popular essays on quirky topics, two successful podcasts, and his online workshop on how to improve as a writer.

## MAKE RULES AND KEEP THEM

Just like hiking on a long trail, pursuing your goal will involve some ambiguity. This can demotivate and slow you down. The antidote is to set up a structure for yourself. Make a rule like "write every day," or "talk to ten new people a week." Then grab a piece of paper, draw a set of blank checkboxes, and mark them off as you complete the tasks. This simple structure of committing to a task and achieving it, repeated over and over, will be the key to your progress toward your goal.

Even if your mountain has deep personal meaning and you have no doubts about it being the right course for you, motivation can be tricky. I'd recommend the simple but powerful "Getting Things Done" method laid out by David Allen. The basic premise is that your brain can't be trusted to focus on the most important things, so instead you can get those decisions out of your brain by writing them down and committing to bite-sized pieces with clear time limits. Such a structure might feel rigid and limiting, but the rules and constraints can provide the perfect backdrop for the kind of ruthless prioritization required to achieve big goals.

## PICK THE RIGHT FRIENDS

The people you are hiking with will have a huge impact on your journey. Imagine hiking alongside someone who complains incessantly, or someone who carelessly steers the group away from the trail. As you Dare Greatly, you want to surround yourself with people who will inspire and motivate you. When combined into a local subculture, a group like this can have an astonishing impact, normalizing the type of achievement that others might assume is impossible.

I've been fortunate to stumble into groups like this throughout my life. I went to a suburban public high school that served middle- to lower middle–class families. These are good people and it's my home community, but the school was not a factory of achievement. There was something special about the group I was lucky enough to join. My friends believed they could accomplish anything, and they put in the work to do it. It was contagious. Watching this group go off to college, enter elite graduate programs, and build lives of purposeful contribution has given me the confidence to set ambitious goals and the support to follow through on them.

My worldview changed again as I arrived at the Massachusetts Institute for Technology and became immersed in the microculture there. MIT students are famous for their "hacks," (usually) innocent but creative pranks that often display some form of engineering prowess. In 2012, some bored students set up a networked array of color-changing LED lights in the 18x9 array of square windows in the Green Building, a twenty-one-story building on campus. The result? A game of Tetris that you could actually play on the side of a highrise building!

There's something different about a group of people who will tackle a project like this. On the one hand, you could call them demented. After all, MIT is not an academic setting where you can sluff off; there are always problem sets to finish, tests to study for, and research to be done. A sane person would focus their limited time and energy on something that "counts," you might argue. But I found this aspect of MIT culture to be exciting. It's powerful. You think of something and figure out how to make it real, not for any reason other than "because you can." And the reason you can do it is because you figured out how. You didn't need anyone's permission. It's a mindset that I found contagious and I've tried to carry with me.

## TAKE OWNERSHIP

There are moments on every long hike where your exhausted body convinces your tired brain that the whole thing was a bad idea. In a clever twist, your brain tells you that hiking this mountain was *someone else's* terrible idea, leading to discouragement, despair, and frustration. You slip into a passive state, going through the motions but without the deliberateness you felt at the beginning. Most people continue to trudge along; others revolt.

But to truly Dare Greatly, you must decide to take ownership. This goal is not forced upon you. You chose it, and you continue to choose it with each step along the way, even when you're tired.

I've had moments where I've done this well, but instead I will share an example of when I completely failed. In eighth grade, I was trying to learn the jungle law of the junior high social system. Misunderstanding how it all worked, I convinced myself that wearing a name brand T-shirt would change my life. The oldest of five kids, I was used to Payless Shoe Store and the sale rack at Kmart. But this was a new year. I was ready to step up my social game, and looking good was the first step. I had my sights set on Mossimo, far and away the coolest brand for kids at my school in 1994. I scrimped and saved, and eventually I was at the mall paying $24 plus tax for a green shirt with the coveted logo scribbled across the front.

I remember putting on the shirt, checking out my reflection, and heading on my bike to school. I remember walking past the lockers and through the halls. I remember watching the other kids for some sort of validation. Suddenly, it hit me. My expensive shirt didn't change one thing about my social status or my life satisfaction. I felt embarrassed for ever having thought it might. In retrospect, I had assigned ownership of my goal to "be cool" away from myself to the Mossimo brand. It didn't work. I had subconsciously allowed my perceptions of the culture around me to set my mountain, and it was the wrong one. Instead of caring what others thought, instead of believing a T-shirt could change my destiny, I wish I had taken ownership of the mountain I was climbing. For example, I could have decided to be a genuine friend to others and to be comfortable with who I am.

## Am I Climbing the Right Mountain?

Hopefully by this point you are excited about the prospect of choosing a mountain and climbing it. I genuinely believe we'd see happier people and a better world if everyone made an effort to Dare Greatly.

But there is one more thing we haven't talked about, and that is when and how to change mountains. After all, pursuing your dreams is a major endeavor that takes all the energy you have, and sometimes more. How do you know if you're climbing the right mountain?

I will propose three tests you can apply to help you know if your chosen mountain is the right one. Before I do that, I want to make two suggestions about the timing of these decisions.

First, climbing the wrong mountain is better than climbing no mountain. This means you should spend less time evaluating and more time climbing, even if you feel very uncertain about whether you will achieve the end goal, or whether you will even want that goal in the end. I'd suggest keeping a mountain defined as your target, and only replacing that mountain when you find another mountain that fits you better.

Second, don't decide on the uphill. At the risk of confusing you by mixing metaphors, I once heard a cross-country runner share a wise insight from her long runs, where muscles ache and bodies feel worn out. There are uphill and downhill portions of the run, and she commits in advance to wait until flat or downhill terrain before making the decision to cut a run short. This still allows for adaptation and flexibility, but prevents our baser human needs in the moment from overriding our true desire.

## CAN'T STOP, WON'T STOP

Test #1: How would you feel if you don't succeed?

If you try hard to accomplish this goal, and somehow it doesn't work out, will you feel like you've wasted your time? Some entrepreneurs are looking for an "exit," a financial transaction where they sell their ownership in the venture they created. This is fine, but risky if this is the only goal, because all startup companies take a ton of work, and only a fraction of them end up with financial success. Big returns are even less likely on a short timescale.

I had an experience a few years ago employing the "what if this fails" test. When I was a kid, my parents bought a kit of plastic pipe toys from the Sears catalog. They were the coolest toy because you could make life-sized forts and tables and towers and cars. We actually melted plastic when we took our gravity-powered homemade car down a steep hill. But these toys were rugged, enduring the bulk of childhood engineering for me and my four siblings over more than a decade of play.

Fast forward to me as a father of four young kids, when I found a wholesaler in Belgium who was keeping hundreds of boxes of these toys in a warehouse. I couldn't believe it. These toys are so fun, and these boxes should be inspiring the next generation of creative future engineers and architects instead of sitting in a warehouse.

Confident that parents and kids would love these toys if I could get them into their hands, I worked out a deal with the Belgian wholesaler and launched a crowdfunding campaign on Indiegogo. It turned into a family affair—my kids in the video, my dad helping me with logistics, and me setting up a steady flow of social media to promote the campaign.

In the end, people were less excited about these toys than I was, and the campaign failed. We didn't get the money. Sadly, the toys are still sitting in a warehouse in Belgium. It was not a success by any measure. Reflecting on the project later, with helpful insights from my wife, I realized that I kind of looked like a crazy person, promoting this weird toy from the 80s with social media posts, even though no one actually wanted them.

Somehow, I just didn't really care. Even though the project failed, I had fun and learned a lot. It was the right mountain for me to climb at the time.

## WHO GETS THE CREDIT?

Test #2: How would you feel if your idea happened, but someone else got the credit for it?

Some Dare Greatly goals exist in a strictly personal realm, like becoming an expert at transcendental meditation, or mastering the complete works of William Shakespeare. But more often, daring greatly involves making a contribution to the world around you. Even in these simple examples of individualistic goals, there could be a collective aspect. For example, becoming a master of meditation could help you bring calm, positive energy to your interactions with others.

One way to test your commitment to the goal you've chosen is to imagine a world where the contribution you have in mind is made, but you personally are not associated with it. How would you feel if other people do the work and get the credit?

During the COVID-19 pandemic, I worked with friends from the local school district to propose a partnership that would allow kids to continue learning through microschools, even when schools were shut down. It was a big lift by many people to create a proposal supported by the academic, finance, and compliance folks in the district. Parents were excited. The final step was school board approval.

I Zoomed into the virtual meeting with the school board, hopeful but unsure what to expect. Over a marathon four-hour session, the school board members started with skeptical questions about the model, but gradually changed their minds as I answered their questions. It seemed like they were seeing how a microschool option could be attractive to parents and an innovative way to empower learners. I allowed myself to feel optimistic!

Then the meeting took an unexpected turn. "We like the concept," the board told me, "but there is no reason we should contract with you to do it. Instead, let's empower the teachers and staff of the district to build our own version of microschools!"

This wasn't what I expected to hear, and honestly, it felt like a punch in the stomach. But after the initial shock, I realized that this could actually be a great thing. Sure, the district running their own microschool program would not contribute to Prenda's business success or do anything for my reputation, but think of the thousands of students that would genuinely love learning in this more flexible way. Think of the engagement, the creativity, the real-world skills!

In the end, I was happy about the decision. I offered to share any resources that might help, at no cost to the district. I continued to support the free pilot program we had started at a Title 1 elementary school. My hope was that kids could become empowered learners, whether or not I got the credit.

## THE RIGHT AMOUNT SCARY

Test #3: Does pursuing the idea feel a little bit scary?

Another way to tell if you are climbing the right mountain is to examine the emotions that come up when you contemplate it. Do you feel excited? Is it uplifting and inspiring you to think about the impact your goal would have on yourself and others? Do you feel some trepidation? I hope so. The most worthwhile goals will stretch you. You may not see the clear path forward. There's a legitimate chance things won't work out the way you want.

I attended a music concert a few years ago in my neighborhood. The program was packed with talent, from nine-year-old violists to adult chamber choral groups. I was enthralled with the performances and grateful for the people that had put in so much work developing talents so that they could share and inspire.

Then I saw a woman in her sixties stand up and walk to the piano. I recognized her, a friend of my parents that I had known for several years. She is a kind neighbor, a loyal friend, and the type of person you just want to be around. But come to think of it, I had never seen her perform any type of music. As it turns out, she did not have an extensive musical background. In the months leading up to this concert, she just decided she wanted to learn the piano, so she went and signed up for lessons.

As I watched her take a seat at the piano, I was nervous with anticipation. She set her hands, took a deep breath, and started to play.

What I heard was pure beauty. Not because she had perfect technique or tackled a famous concerto—she stumbled through a simple song—but because she was Daring Greatly.

I thought about all the lessons, waiting for her turn while the piano teacher finished up with the eight-year-old student right before. I thought about the worries she might have had, about what her family and friends might think. I imagined the internal narrative, accusing herself of being too old to learn piano. And now, here she was, in front of an entire audience, on the program with more polished performances, and taking on her fear headfirst. What a beautiful example of Daring Greatly.

# Daring Greatly in Action:

**WHAT'S YOUR NEXT MOUNTAIN TO CLIMB?**

Are you currently working toward a big goal? Maybe it's written on a notecard, taped to your bathroom mirror. Or maybe it's part of your morning meditation routine. If you have a mountain clearly in mind and you're on your way to climbing it, skip to the next question.

If not, it's time to choose a mountain. In his book *Dream Big*, author Bob Goff gives three simple questions that can help you pick the right mountain. I'd recommend sitting down in a quiet spot and writing down ideas that come to you as you contemplate your answers to these questions.

- Who are you?

- Where are you?

- What do you want?

Once you've considered this, ask yourself what actions will get you closer to that goal?

Once you know what you want and feel confident, the next step is to take some actions. Don't worry if your list is complete, or if it feels overwhelming. Just write down the things you can do to move yourself up the mountain. Make sure to add "due dates" to make sure you keep moving. Hold yourself accountable. Find other people that can help you succeed.

Questions to consider continuously to Dare Greatly:

- What would I want said about me at my funeral?

- What's a goal inside that big vision?

- Why do I want to pursue this goal?

- If someone else achieved the outcome, would I be happy?

- Does this goal excite me and scare me a bit?

- Do I have an action plan to make this goal happen?

- Are there people around me who also Dare Greatly?

- What in my environment needs to change to support what I'm up to?

- Am I owning my life right now?

# Dare Greatly Vignette:

# Carla's Story

I STOOD IN A NONDESCRIPT SUBURBAN PARKING LOT ON THE EDGE OF town, waiting for my ride to pick me up, nervous and excited for the day ahead. The weather was cool, the skies mostly blue with a few lazy clouds. I was preparing for my first visit to San Carlos, Arizona, a small community in Eastern Arizona that is home to the San Carlos Apache tribe. As a lifelong resident of Arizona, I had long been aware of the various Indigenous groups that traced their local roots back much earlier than my European ancestors arriving in the area. I had had limited exposure to Native communities across the state and formed a few friendships with tribal members from the Navajo, Hopi, Pima, and other communities.

Today was a trip east, where a friend was introducing me to his extended family, the stewards of a church in San Carlos. We were meeting families from the community and exploring the possibility of opening a microschool.

Schools in San Carlos were struggling. In the local school district, more than half of kids do not graduate from high school, test scores are very low, and advanced courses are virtually unavailable. Things didn't seem to improve with more funding, as the district spends nearly $20,000 per student per year, more than double the Arizona average of $8,000. The two parochial schools in town had long waiting lists, and many parents and guardians were looking for options.

Of course, the challenges in the education system are symptomatic of other, deeper hardships. Poverty, addiction, limited economic opportunities, and other problems make it difficult for young people in San Carlos to even consider Daring Greatly. So as the families wandered in, I had no idea what to expect.

I met a group of three girls, around eleven or twelve years old. They lived with an elderly grandmother and attended the local elementary school. As I greeted them and learned a little about them, I noticed their unflinching politeness and a look of skepticism on their faces. I imagine it could be a little strange, hearing this white guy from Phoenix talk about a new way of doing school.

One of the girls—I'll call her Carla—mentioned that she enjoys math but hasn't been doing very much of it recently. I opened up a laptop and showed her the self-paced lessons in Khan Academy. She started answering a few math questions, and when it was clear that she understood one topic, she moved to the next one in line.

After twenty minutes or so, I stopped by the table where Carla was working. It was fascinating to see the confidence and energy she radiated. She'd already knocked off a good portion of her grade level in math, and she was diving into the next lessons. I pointed out her affinity for math, and she smiled modestly, but then her outlook changed. With hopeful incredulity, she asked if she could just keep going like this? Could she really learn all the math she wanted? She didn't need to wait for anyone to give her permission?

It was a moment of Daring Greatly. I could see in Carla's eyes that she had found an inner excitement and enthusiasm for math. She was ready to choose it as her mountain to climb, and already started taking the small steps that would bring her where she wanted to be.

I showed her how to move from one lesson to the next, moving ahead to the next grade level when she mastered the current one. I pointed out that the math in Khan Academy goes all the way into college, covering the basic concepts behind science, finance, engineering, and many other possible trajectories.

Carla signed up for the microschool, and with the support and help from her learning guide, her friends in the class, and others from the community, she embarked on a quest to become great at math.

# Chapter 3

# Figure It Out

IN APRIL 1970, AN EXPLOSION ON THEIR SPACECRAFT CREATED AN emergency situation for the three astronauts on the Apollo 13 mission. Instead of landing on the moon as scheduled, the crew was forced to crowd into a tiny lunar module for survival. The plan was a slingshot course around the moon and back to Earth.

Somewhere in the middle of their 142-hour journey, the ground crew in Houston realized for the second time that "we have a problem." The Lunar Module was designed to sustain life for a shorter time period, but now it was the lifeboat that would carry the astronauts to safety. As it turned out, there was plenty of oxygen for them to breathe in, but the carbon dioxide they exhaled into the small space was gradually making the air poisonous. As Captain Jim Lovell put it, "we would have died of the exhaust from our own lungs if Mission Control hadn't come up with a marvelous fix."

There is a canister in the Lunar Module designed to absorb extra carbon dioxide out of the air. But with all three of them breathing, the filter was saturating and losing its ability to function, creating a dangerous situation. The folks at Mission Control realized that there were some backup canisters in the other part of the ship, but they were shaped like a square, and the slot for the canister in the Lunar Module was a circle. It was the literal manifestation of a "square peg in a round hole."

What happens in a situation like this? Three lives on the line, emergency conditions, the whole world watching. Everything has gone wrong, off the plan, outside the design conditions. If you've seen the movie *Apollo 13*, you might remember the dramatic moment when the engineers stand around a table looking at a pile of random supplies that would be available for the astronauts to craft a makeshift solution. Cut to the next scene, where the ground is radioing instructions to use the cardboard from the flight manual, some extra tubing, and duct tape to build a life-saving converter.

The collaboration between the astronauts on Apollo 13 and the engineers and technicians on the ground is one of my favorite illustrations of human beings taking on a learning challenge and succeeding. It's a dramatic, high-stakes example of the next core value: Figure It Out.

Now contrast that with the way most of us interact with learning today. I saw firsthand how badly the world needs a Figure It Out mentality one day in the afterschool Code Club program I ran at the public library.

It was a typical Monday afternoon, and a horde of children was rolling into the conference room. Most of them were regulars who knew the drill: meet me in the corner to get a laptop, then find an open spot at a table, check the "challenge of the day" written on the whiteboard, and get to work coding. It was loud and busy, and a lot of fun.

The class was twenty minutes into session by the time I finished all the start-up errands. I looked up and noticed one of the new kids still sitting politely at his computer. He was staring straight ahead, just sitting there with hands folded neatly in his lap.

I remembered meeting him a few minutes earlier when his mom dropped him off. He was hiding behind her leg, tentative about meeting me, and looking around the energetic room with a nervous excitement. I said hello, got him a computer, and introduced him to a buddy who could help him get started.

Noticing him now, I realized that he was not used to the way things worked at Code Club. Instead of diving into the self-paced tutorials, he was waiting for a lesson. Instead of starting on a project, he was waiting for an assignment. Instead of asking the other kids what was going on, he was obeying the rule of keeping to yourself. He was expecting education to happen to him. But at Code Club, we Figure It Out. It wasn't his fault; he hadn't seen a setting like this before.

Fast forward two months, when I saw this same kid, but the situation was completely different. He had been coming every week, picking up the Figure It Out mentality. Now he was one of the crazy kids that showed up and knew exactly how to get started. He had projects he was obsessed with finishing. The other kids were asking him questions. His smile was ear to ear, reflecting the confidence and joy of a learner in his element.

## Not as Obvious as It Seems

Figure It Out is at the very center of the empowered learner lifestyle. It's about asking good questions, devouring sources of information, and taking as many repeated attempts as it takes to master something. Does this seem obvious? How else could learning happen?

You'd be surprised.

One of the software tools Prenda students used to use is Khan Academy. With a complete library of math content and constant quizzing to test for mastery, a student in Khan Academy is working right at their learning frontier. In theory, you're never lost or struggling to comprehend what the class is working on. In theory, you're also never bored, repeating exercises on a topic you already understand. It has the potential for very efficient learning. But it doesn't always go that way.

If you answer a question correctly, the program congratulates you and you move on to the next one. If you miss it, the program offers three optional ways to help you learn: a text-based hint, a video tutorial, and a step-by-step walkthrough of the problem. Together, these options provide a perfect pathway to get unstuck, right in the moment. But if you watch kids using the program, they don't always accept the offer.

I've spent a lot of time watching kids in Khan Academy. So often, they respond to a missed question with the opposite of Figure It Out! Sometimes they stare blankly at the screen or divert their attention somewhere else in the room, escaping from the pain of not understanding. Sometimes they click the button that says "Skip to the next question," missing the chance to learn from the mistake. Worse, many of the kids will start guessing on the remaining questions, eliminating the possibility of learning. Part of the reason for this is plain and simple psychology; learning hurts, and there is always an easier path available. We'll dig into this deeper in the next chapter, where I introduce the value of Learning > Comfort.

Part of the reason is a rational response to the rules of the game. In Khan Academy, the goal is mastery, measured by a consecutive string of correct answers on a specific topic. Let's say you partially understand a concept, and the first three problems are the type you know how to solve. Now you arrive at the fourth problem, and it looks a little different. It's just on the other side of your learning frontier. You have every incentive to try hard to answer this problem correctly, but you get the answer wrong despite your best efforts. Travesty! Your string of correct answers is broken, and you no longer have the chance to sign off this topic and advance in your mastery measurement. This is the moment when the temptation sets in. If you just click through the rest of the questions, you can get a fresh start and maybe next time convince the computer that you have mastered the topic.

The problem with this all-too-common sequence? It is not learning! It's like a hungry person running past tables full of food without stopping to eat. Instead of mindlessly racing through problems, I coach kids to adopt a Figure It Out mentality. You missed a question? Great! Each wrong answer is an opportunity to learn. Slow down, review the concept, read the hint, walk through the problem with help, and make sure you understand the gap in your knowledge. If you clearly understand why you missed the problem, you can fill in the learning gap and get it right, not just the next time, but in all future problems.

When you're living the value of Figure It Out, you care less about the outcome of each specific problem and more about the learning underneath. If you guess correctly, but don't really understand the concept, you're not satisfied. If you get the answer wrong but learn from it, you're delighted.

## GOTTA GET YOUR MIND RIGHT

My neighbor was a detective for the local police department, at the tail end of a long career. He was a man of few words, but he had all kinds of interesting stories, so I was constantly trying to get him talking.

Once he described a tense situation where he had to coach some junior officers before entering an engagement. He invoked a line from the 1967 film, *Cool Hand Luke*, advising his colleagues: "You gotta get your mind right." He wanted to make sure that each individual was in the proper frame of mind, knowing that their internal narratives and unconscious assumptions could make the difference between success and failure. Even though I haven't seen the movie and I'm pretty sure the context of the quote is completely different, the concept has stuck with me. Whether in policing, solving math problems, mentoring children, learning a sport or musical instrument, launching a new organization, or anything else you want to do, your *mindset* will be a key determinant of your success.

When it comes to the power of mindset in learning endeavors, there's no one more helpful than Carol Dweck, a pioneering psychologist and author of the book *Mindset*. The framing is simple: you can believe one of two things about your brain and its capacity to learn.

1. A fixed mindset assumes intelligence and talents are stable and unchanging, set by nature and outside of your control. "I'm not a math person," you might say, implying that somewhere inside your genetic material is a chain of proteins that will prevent you from learning math, no matter how much you try.

2. A growth mindset assumes the opposite, that your "most basic abilities can be developed through dedication and hard work—brains and talent are just the starting point. This view creates a love of learning and a resilience that is essential for great accomplishment."[12]

Getting your mind right for learning requires a growth mindset. We'll dive deeper in the next chapter, Learning > Comfort. For now, I invite you to get curious about your own beliefs. The home page for the Khan Academy used to have a headline I found incredibly powerful: "You can learn anything." The punctuation was a simple period, as if this incredibly bold statement is just plain truth.

---

[12] "Growth Mindset," The Glossary of Education Reform, last updated August 29, 2013, https://www.edglossary.org/growth-mindset/.

Do you believe that you can learn anything? If you're coaching, teaching, or mentoring another human, do you believe that they can learn anything? I believe this is true, but that doesn't matter. What matters is that you believe it.

## INFORMATION AT YOUR FINGERTIPS

At a computer hacker conference in 1984, Stewart Brand spawned a whole movement (and later, an associated controversy) by declaring that "information wants to be free." This was the dawn of the information age, with computers just becoming accessible to regular people, but before the widespread connectivity of the internet. I remember those days. I was just a kid, but I vividly remember the IBM machine my dad brought home, with the clunky CRT monitor displaying green text on a black background. I learned how to navigate the DOS prompt and create a digital file I could go back and edit later. For the first time, ordinary folk like me could separate the information and ideas from the physical containers that held them, like books and newspapers.

To illustrate just how revolutionary this was, let's go back in time over 2,000 years and visit the Great Library of Alexandria, in the west end of the Nile River delta in Egypt. Through a variety of means, some more ethical than others, the Ptolemaic Kingdom had amassed a collection of tens of thousands of papyrus scrolls, representing the collective writings of civilization. Some estimate that this collection was the equivalent of around 100,000 books today. If you lived at the turn of the millennium and wanted to understand a topic that your immediate family and neighbors did not know about, the only way to learn it was to travel hundreds or thousands of miles by land or by sea, then convince the scholars at the library to let you in. Virtually impossible for all but a very small few.

Contrast that with today. Something interesting comes up in a conversation and you want to know more. Who is the oldest person to play professional basketball? How do I apply consistent formatting to the headings in Google Docs? You're seconds away from the Wikipedia page, or a YouTube video with step-by-step instructions. Vast quantities of information on an endless array of topics, all on your phone or laptop. There is still a digital divide and significant progress to be made expanding access, but for most people reading this book, access to information is no longer the limiting factor for human learning.

This is an exciting time to embrace the Figure It Out approach.

## How to "Figure It Out"

If lack of information is no longer the limitation to powerful learning, then what is? What is stopping people from embarking on regular learning quests, tackling new content, picking up new skills, and building new things?

One way to look at this question is to view learning as a recipe, with each ingredient playing a critical part. We've already talked about Daring Greatly, connecting the gritty day-to-day of learning with a higher purpose or personal meaning. Without a sense of purpose, real learning does not happen, any more than a loaf of sourdough bread can happen without yeast. Later, we will explore the interpersonal relationships with other humans that can help or hinder learning. These factors are like the warm water and the hot oven, unlocking the chemical reactions that turn raw ingredients into delicious bread.

"Figure It Out" is like the flour in the bread recipe. It's the substance of the learning, from embracing the steps to seeking out the information that will help you achieve your goal. A college student might think of these activities in terms of

**enrollment** (signing up for a specific course in a specific major, offered by a specific professor), **curriculum** (a list of the lectures, assignments, quizzes, etc. that lead to understanding of the topic), and **assessment** (a test score or grade proving that you learned the content of the course). But Figuring It Out extends far beyond a formal institution; anyone who wants to learn anything must decide on the steps that will lead to learning, make a commitment, and follow through.

The concepts of enrollment, curriculum, and assessment show up in every learning situation.

Let's say you are hearing a squeaking noise from the front brakes on your car. You are still emotionally scarred by the bill from the last time you visited the mechanic, and you remember hearing a friend explain how he changed the brake pads on his car. Maybe you could save some money, learn something new, and look tough with car grease on your hands. You enroll when you decide to give it a go. Your curriculum starts with a phone call to that friend, who walks you through the basics and offers to lend you some tools. You find a tutorial on YouTube and watch it a couple times before you go outside, set up the car jack, and start raising the car. When you try to loosen the lug nuts to remove the tire, they won't budge, so you call the friend again and he reminds you that you have to "break" the seal on the bolts while the car is still on the ground. You sigh, then begin twisting the jack the other way until the car is back down to where it started. Now you grab the wrench, line it up the right direction, and push down with your foot until you feel it move. Four more times, and you're ready to raise the car again, and this time you have no trouble loosening the lug nuts and taking off the wheel. The process continues for a couple of messy, sweaty hours. The slider bolt and caliper are easy, the good folks at the auto shop have no trouble getting you the replacement pads, you have to read a couple articles online to figure out how to retract the pistons, and finally you put everything back together, checking twice to make sure your handiwork is functional, especially for something as life-or-death as brakes. You've completed the course, and you ask your friendly neighbor to double-check your work before you put the wheel back and start your test drive. You don't crash, so you've passed the course. Congratulations!

You could find a similar learning adventure in anything meaningful or worthwhile.

- Picking up a basic level of understanding in a foreign language through study, practice, and immersion.

- Tackling a musical instrument, learning the fundamentals, practicing scales, painstakingly reading the notes of a song before eventually mastering the piece and performing it for others.

- Asking honest questions and listening to understand the underlying issues in a marriage or other relationship, then engaging in uncomfortable conversations, enlisting the help of an outside expert, and working with your partner to make things better.

- Changing careers as a middle-aged adult, working through months of embarrassing conversations, challenging course-work, and vulnerable resume submissions.

- Signing up for a sport you have never played before and spending hours doing drills, incorporating feedback from coaches, and competing when you don't feel ready.

- Starting a business based on a hobby you're passionate about and meticulously preparing all the details before awkwardly offering your goods or services for sale.

- Pursuing an interest in painting, sculpting, pottery, or any form of artistic expression, putting in the hours to acquire technique and then breaking the rules as you take risks.

- Launching a nonprofit organization to support a cause you care about, learning the administrative steps, raising money, managing a budget, leading people, and seeing your impact in small and large ways.

This list could go on forever. I am not trying to give you a mountain to climb; only you can do that. What I want you to see is that no matter the mountain, the steps toward learning are in your grasp.

## HIDING PLACES

This emphasis on learning might feel obvious, but if you look around a typical school or workplace, you will notice that Figure It Out mindsets are rare. Why? As we'll talk about in the next chapter, learning is uncomfortable. It's always easier not to do it. And there are plenty of places to hide.

Let's walk through a few of the most common ways we avoid learning. This list of hiding places is not exhaustive; there are many more ways to duck the discomfort. And it's not that these things are inherently evil; the danger lies in anything we turn to to escape the challenge and scariness of the messy learning process.

## LOOSE ACCOUNTABILITY

Even when we are operating at our psychological best, with a pure desire for learning and improving, we struggle with the follow through. Think of all the well-intentioned plans to eat better, to exercise more, or to wake up earlier. We know these things will help us become the person we want to be, and yet we struggle anyway.

In its ideal form, accountability is the connection between our rational selves and the immediate whims of the moment. The best accountability comes from within, connected to the purpose and goal you set when daring greatly. But even the best intentions will not lead to results, as any book in the self-help section will tell you. You need to make a plan and stick to it.

Runners are more likely to prepare for a marathon when they schedule times with a running buddy. Dieters are more likely to stick to the plan if they track what they ate in an app or journal. Sleepers are more likely to wake up early if they set their alarm the night before. (If you really want to wake up, get an alarm without a snooze button. Or you could try Clocky, the cute robotic alarm that allows you to hit snooze, but then moves to a random spot in your room and sounds the alarm again.)

Psychologist Dan Ariely is an expert in the myriad ways that our automatic brains undermine our rational thinking. Many of the examples in his book *Predictably Irrational* are directly or indirectly related to the human quest for learning.

I saw one example of this firsthand, during the early days of the afterschool Code Club program. In 2013 when we started, there was a burgeoning list of online resources for people who wanted to learn how to code. Many of them, like Scratch and FreeCodeCamp.org, were free to everyone, and many others offered a portion of their content for free. I didn't even try to design my own learn-to-code curriculum. Instead, I pointed kids to these resources and encouraged them to work their way through tutorials. Eventually, my friends and I created a software app that provided scaffolding for the content and accountability for learners to measure their progress.

As you know, Code Club was very popular among families from all demographics, with many of them driving a long time to get there. What astonished me was that we were using content from the internet. These kids could have done these tutorials from home! Why were they coming to Code Club? One reason was accountability. In our fun app, featuring workouts and missions and avatars decked out with incredible virtual gear, kids found a structure that helped them see their progress toward the bigger goal of learning to code.


## CREDENTIALISM

Another place to hide from the tough work of Figuring It Out is behind a degree, certificate, or other credential. On the surface, the idea of a credential makes perfect sense. I received specialized training, I put in the time and effort, and a trusted entity granted me a bona fide certificate for all the world to see. This is all great, and I have no problem at all with the pursuit of knowledge through formal programs.

The problem comes when a credential becomes a hiding place, inducing complacency and getting in the way of the ongoing learning. For example, someone might graduate from a prestigious college with an honors degree and find that they have an easy time getting job interviews. But that same person could be surprised if they find that getting and keeping a job depends on how they do at the job. Even more surprising to some, the demands of the work almost never maps to the content from the classroom. So success depends on the ability to learn, long after graduation. Regardless of the degree hanging on the wall, those who can set goals and learn how to accomplish them are equipped for success. On the other hand, those who believe that everything will come easy because of their academic training are in for a shock. A comical example of this is Andy Bernard from the TV show *The Office*, who annoys everyone by constantly gloating about his alma mater, Cornell University.

Comedians have been poking fun at credentialism for decades. In a 1978 episode of *Saturday Night Live*, Bill Murray is carted into the office of a medieval barber after a terrible accident. Keeping with the medical traditions of his day, the barber prescribes a round of bloodletting, to which the patient complains, "But I'm bleeding already!" The punchline encapsulates the idea of credentialism: "Say, who's the barber here?"

The institution of tenure can be a form of credentialism. I remember showing up at college with an interest in computer programming. I took the intro level course, which was held in a huge lecture hall. The course was taught in the Java programming language, despite the already widespread adoption of more modern languages in the broader world. Wondering why the course was clinging to technology that added unnecessary stumbling blocks (I still don't fully understand exactly what "public static void main" means), I realized that Java was the language the professor was most comfortable with, and because he had the credential of "tenured faculty," he had no real incentive to reexamine the decision. After all, changing the language of the course curriculum would require a lot of learning and effort, Java is still suitable, and the class had been going just fine for many semesters before. I should mention here that even though I eked out an A minus in the course, grumbled a lot, and decided against a computer science major as a result of this experience, I later realized that the specific programming language doesn't matter as much as the concepts underneath.

More than being a hiding place, credentialism can show up as a counterfeit to the Figure It Out value, acting in direct opposition. In a past life, I was working with a leader who was turning out to be a poor fit for the company. I liked this person a lot, and he had the respect of many of the people on his team and across the organization, but for some reason I couldn't quite put my finger on, there was a growing tension in our interactions. We talked about it, and he was able to express some of the frustration in terms of the challenges he received from me and others. He felt annoyed that he had to explain and justify his recommendations, because he was speaking from a position of deep expertise on the topic. He had done comparable work in other places. He had an advanced degree in the field. He frequently cited articles, books, and TED Talks that propounded the frameworks. In this person's mind, he had already "figured it out," and everyone around him was betraying the ideal when they engaged and debated instead of accepting his perspective as the "expert opinion." It's easy to see how this makes perfect sense; I'd be frustrated too! On the other hand, Figure It Out means approaching every situation with an openness and eagerness to get to the best solution. Bring the paradigms and experiences you've already accumulated, but don't be surprised when each new situation needs a fresh application.

**JARGON**
Using fancy technical terms and industry-specific terminology is another way we sometimes hide from learning. Language can either clarify or obscure the ideas behind it. But if we are not sure about the underlying concept and want to seem smart anyway, throwing out jargon is a great way to do it.

When I was a teenager, my brother and I bought a record of Steve Martin standup comedy. The records were $1 each, stacked unceremoniously in a cardboard box on the floor of the pet store. We recognized Steve Martin from his roles in such

classics as *The Three Amigos* and we were excited to buy the record
and give it a listen.

There's a moment on the album where Steve mentions a
plumbing convention in town, saying a bunch of plumbers were
attending the show that night. He tells the audience that he has
prepared a special joke for the plumbers, and to please bear with
him. Then he adopts a ridiculously serious tone of voice and
launches into the bit:

> This lawn supervisor is out on a sprinkler maintenance
> job, and he starts working on a Finley sprinkler head with
> a Langstrom seven-inch gangley wrench. The apprentice
> leans over and says, "You can't work on a Finley head
> with a Langstrom seven-inch wrench!" Well this infu-
> riated the supervisor, so he went and got Volume 14 of
> the Kingsley manual. He reads to the apprentice, saying
> "the Langstrom seven-inch wrench can be used with the
> Finley sprocket." Just then, the apprentice leans toward
> him and says, "It says sprocket, not socket!"[13]

Of course he's completely lost his audience, and his awkward chuckle is the only laughter in the house. Realizing this
and pretending to feel stupid, Steve lands the actual punchline,
muttering to someone offstage: "Are those plumbers supposed
to be here this show, or the next one?"

This is funny because we can all relate to the feeling of listening to someone talk, but having no idea what they are talking
about because of the language they are choosing. We may default
to the assumption that the speaker really knows their stuff and
everyone else understands perfectly because "they are smart and
I am not." But in fact, jargon is often how people hide their

---

[13] Steve Martin, "Let's Get Small," track 3 on *Let's Get Small*, Warner Brothers, 1977, LP.

own poor understanding of underlying concepts—and we've all done it.

Technical jargon, acronyms, and other insider lingo can save time and build cohesion among a tight-knit group; there's nothing wrong with it on its face. But too often, it becomes a hiding place that gets in the way of figuring it out. Because I decided a long time ago to disregard feeling dumb and just ask questions until I understand what people are talking about, I have learned that most of the time, jargon is deliberate ambiguity masking unclear understanding or unformed ideas.

This stood out the clearest when I was taking a class in plasma physics at MIT. It was all about the complicated motion of electrons inside of a nuclear fusion reactor. Imagine tiny charged particles responding to powerful magnetic fields, swirling around and bumping into each other. I was intimidated as all get out, knowing that my professor literally wrote the book and was recognized as a world expert, with the publications and awards to prove it. If ever there was a time for jargon, this was it. And yet, instead, I listened to this professor explain things like "banana orbits" and "sausage instabilities," invoking the shape of foods to provide a clear picture of a complicated phenomenon. He had mastered the topic, understood it so deeply he could communicate it in simple language, and he had nothing to prove.

Think of the myriad ways you hear technical jargon. From the personal trainer at the gym talking about 1RM or cluster sets, to the marketing wizard referencing CPC and CTA, to the IT consultant warning about DDoS attacks and phishing, dropping technical jargon to a layperson has the same effect: making them look like an expert and intimidating others into silently questioning their own intellectual capacity.

**FORMULAE**

Finish this sentence: a squared plus b squared equals _____.
What about this one? The area of a circle equals pi times _____.
Do you remember these formulas from math class? Do you
remember what they mean? Have you ever thought about why
they work?

Probably not, according to mathematician and author Paul
Lockhart. After years as a research mathematician at top tier uni-
versities, followed by more years teaching math to high school
kids, Professor Lockhart wrote a book called *A Mathematician's
Lament*, published in 2009. His core argument is that most
people experience math as a series of formulas to memorize without ever acknowledging the beauty and wonder of the underlying
concepts. "The first thing to understand is that mathematics
is an art," he explains, but "The difference between math and
other arts…is that our culture does not recognize it as such."[14]

Why would educators and students ignore the fun parts
and turn math into a chore? Why do we have a generation of
adults where a majority believes "I'm not a math person?" The
short answer is that it's easier to follow a formula. It provides a
comfortable hiding place from the risk and effort required to
Figure It Out.

We see the same thing in cooking. It's relatively easy to follow
a recipe: mix these ingredients in this order, apply heat in this way,
and voilà! But as any chef will tell you, the joy of the culinary arts
lies beyond the recipe, where an intuitive understanding of the
subtle tastes and textures of each ingredient opens up a universe
of exploration and improvisation, leading to delicious new flavors.

Where else do we find the temptation to hide from learning
behind an accepted formula? It turns out that we do it all the
time!

---

[14] Paul Lockhart, *A Mathematician's Lament: How School Cheats Us Out of Our Most
Fascinating and Imaginative Art Form* (New York: Bellevue Literary Press, 2009), 22.

- Attend a four-year university, invoking substantial personal debt, even though your interests do not line up with the degree programs available.

- Stick with a job you hate because you only have seven years left until retirement and a pension.

- Limit your job search to online resume submissions, even though you know that meeting people in the industry will be helpful.

- Spend all of your time as an entrepreneur trying to raise money and get press instead of building something useful.

- Engage with other professionals in your field in a trans-actional way, accumulating business cards instead of connecting as humans.

There are useful heuristics and helpful wisdom behind most formulas. The ideas in my list above are not all bad (some are). The point is that clinging to the formula will not get you where you want to go. Formulas promise a convenient shortcut, but we know deep down that there is a better way. Sometimes we just need the courage to change course.

One of my favorite themes in the education innovation world is the idea that every learner is different, that there is not one standard path for everyone, and that anyone can learn new skills. For example, Propel America helps high school graduates enter healthcare careers, Degreed helps upskill people on the job, and a variety of "bootcamp" programs help adults enter technical fields. In each case, people are realizing that the formula they bought into might not be right for them, and there is learning and growth in the free space outside the formula.

## An Experiment about Mindset

I went to college with a guy named Mark Rober, who at the time was a strong engineering student with a great sense of humor and a penchant for clever pranks. Over time, Mark built a following online, starting with tech-enabled Halloween costumes, and today he is among the YouTube elite, delighting millions with science and engineering videos like "Egg Drop from Space."

In a talk called "The Super Mario Effect," Mark points out that the only difference between memorizing a random sequence of button presses and rescuing Princess Peach from the evil Bowser is the story—an arbitrary meaning our brains assign to the inputs and outputs of reality. So much of our approach to life and learning is the framing. How do we make sense of our effort? Is it monotonous drudgery, or are we experiencing the thrill of Figuring It Out?[15]

Even though I'm not a famous YouTuber, I had the chance to "collab" with Mark on an interesting research project that sheds more light on the Figure It Out mentality. With help from coding genius Andy Jennings and behavioral economist Ty Turley, we designed an experiment. We created a coding puzzle where the player uses logic blocks like "move forward one step" and "repeat x times" to move a car through a maze. You win if you get the car to the end of the maze. Mark sent this puzzle to his subscribers, and 50,000 people attempted to solve it.

The players would click the logic blocks together in whatever configuration they wanted, and we measured each time they clicked the "run" button, noting whether their code got the car to the end of the maze. We also tracked the total points of each player; more points meant a higher chance of winning an iPad in a random drawing from the pool of everyone who solved the

---

[15] TEDx Talks, "The Super Mario Effect - Tricking Your Brain into Learning More | Mark Rober | TEDxPenn," May 31, 2018, YouTube video, 15:08, https://www.youtube.com/watch?v=9vJRopau0g0.

puzzle. The experiment was to see if we could nudge the way people approached the problem. We varied two things:

1. The messaging people received after they hit the "run" button and saw the result. Some people received positive messages, encouraging them to keep trying. Others got neutral messages, just saying if they were successful or not. The final group was negative messaging, like, "That's gotta hurt. You failed."

2. The rules of the game. Half the participants were given "School rules," penalized for wrong answers (minus five points) and the other half, with what we called "Mastery rules," were not penalized.

Which variable do you expect had the biggest impact? If you were trying to solve this puzzle, would the messages matter? What about the points?

It was interesting to analyze the results. Because so many people attempted the puzzle, we were able to see small and large effects, all with statistical significance because tens of thousands of people tried the puzzle. Here's what we found:

- Messaging matters. People who saw positive messages, reinforcing a growth mindset and encouraging them to keep trying, were about 5 percentage points more likely to solve the puzzle.

- Rules matter more. There was a much larger gap tied to the structure of the game. Those who were not penalized for wrong answers were 16 percentage points more likely to solve the puzzle.

Here are the results for all six "buckets."

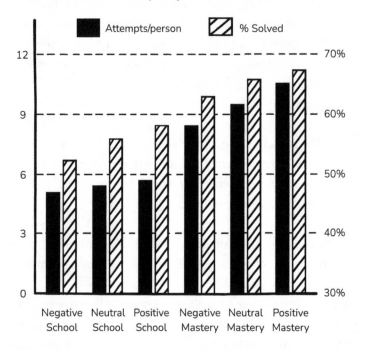

## Puzzle results by experimental bucket

Another thing we noticed in these results was persistence. Those who solved the puzzle successfully clicked the "run" button a lot of times. Most people that quit after two or three attempts did not solve the puzzle. More attempts, with learning from each failure in between, correlates to more success.

What is the main takeaway? Learning is hard and messy, and the best piece of advice is to stick with it. As long as you don't quit, as long as you can learn from each failed attempt, you will get there eventually. This may not be true in a locked down classroom where notes, calculators, Google searches, and talking to peers are considered cheating. But everywhere else in the world, the main thing is to keep trying until you Figure It Out.

In our efforts as individual learners, and in our quest to help others learn, the primary focus should be supporting and reinforcing this mindset. Learning should feel like a game we want to win, and the setbacks and failures along the way are all part of the process. "Focus on the princess and not the pits," Mark says. Compared to the carrots, sticks, and other Pavlovian devices imposed on us by others, a real desire to learn is incredibly powerful as a motivator. It's a game we choose to play.

## INTRINSIC MOTIVATION

Researchers refer to a deep personal desire for learning as intrinsic motivation. It's the gold standard in getting ourselves to choose action over inaction, persistence over quitting.

Intrinsic motivation comes from a clear vision for the future and a connection between the struggles of today and the outcomes of tomorrow. Prenda students do this with an activity called "Future You," where each child creates a visual representation of themselves, thirty years in the future. It's fascinating to see what they come up with: watercolors of dancers, collages of engineers, pencil sketches of happy dog owners. After finishing their artwork, the kids have a make-believe conversation with the future version of themselves. They revel in imagination, dreaming about how amazing their life will be. They explore the path their future self took to get to such a great spot, noticing the hard work they put in along the way. The final question in this conversation with their future self, and my favorite part, is where the child asks: "What could I do now to help me become this person?"

## High Demand for "Figure It Out"

The world is facing a serious shortage of people who live the value of "Figure It Out." As a result, those who master this approach become every employer's dream.

In the early days of Code Club, I spent time meeting with local business leaders to raise money for our program. I met executives, engineers, and many other professionals from the leading firms in the area.

One day I stopped into a particularly swanky office in Scottsdale, Arizona, to ask for a check. It was home to one of the most respected, most successful law firms in the state. Picture floor-to-ceiling glass, expensive-looking modern furniture, abstract art on the walls, and smart, powerful people in fancy suits and polished shoes. My meeting was with the senior partners, one of whose names was on the building.

Taking a deep breath to settle my nerves, I explained how Code Club works. I walked them through the learning software, giving them a chance to try out some basic coding. The four of us were gathered around my laptop, cracking up as they solved puzzles and customized a simple video game. They experienced the Figure It Out approach firsthand, taking risks and supporting each other through repeated failures. As the significance of this learning approach sunk in, one of the partners stopped me mid-sentence.

She explained her role as a senior partner at the firm, responsible for the recruiting and onboarding of new lawyers. She explained the academic pedigree and abnormal intelligence of the fresh associates. They came from top law schools. They had high LSAT scores and GPAs. They had stellar resumes filled with community service and extracurricular activities. But there was something wrong. I could see the anguish in her face as she talked about the problem that was stressing her out. These young lawyers didn't know how to Figure It Out!

A new associate gets assigned to his first case, carrying a pile of brown accordion file folders back to his desk with a determined look on his face. He starts researching the key issues, documenting sources, and crafting arguments. It all feels like a case from law school...until it doesn't. *This wasn't included in my training! There is no clear, predefined way to think about this. What do I do?* This worry led the new associates back to the senior partner's office, asking for more direction. It happened all the time, and she was frazzled.

As we sat there together in this fancy boardroom, this thousand-dollar-an-hour partner saw something in the coding puzzles we give to eight-year-olds. It was a fresh approach to solving problems that involved courage, resourcefulness, and creativity. "If all my junior associates did this program, I genuinely believe they would be better lawyers." Although we ultimately decided against it, this partner seriously considered adding a mandatory coding curriculum as part of the onboarding for new lawyers, not because of the technical skills, but as a training ground for a Figure It Out mentality.

## The Three Questions

How do you know if you're applying a Figure It Out mentality? It can be tricky. Sometimes we stay stuck in a rut, determined to do it ourselves with no help. Sometimes we use other people as a crutch, following the path of least resistance to get the immediate task done without actually learning it ourselves.

At Prenda, we train adults to ask kids a progression of three simple questions. These may seem obvious, but you'd be surprised how frequently the process is a revelatory experience. Each question is designed to invite the learner to take ownership of the learning and to reinforce the Figure It Out process.

When someone is stuck and raises their hand to ask for help, I walk up with a smile and ask the first question.

## 1. WHAT HAVE YOU TRIED SO FAR?

We start with an open question, inviting the learner to reflect on the attempts they have made so far. If you've spent time around young people, it might not surprise you that most of the time, the answer is nothing. A kid would get stuck on a math problem or coding exercise, sit there, look at it, and then raise their hand. They sometimes seemed startled with my question. *What do you mean? I was supposed to do something? I thought I sit here and you teach me?* If they haven't yet made an effort, I would point them to a tutorial or video lesson, smile, and walk away. The goal was not to be harsh, but to land the message that learning is not a thing that happens to you as you sit waiting.

After a while, this idea sinks in, and I get called over to help someone who is already actively engaged in learning. I ask the same question, and the child launches into an explanation of what they are trying to do, and all the ways that haven't worked yet. Sometimes, halfway through the explanation, a light bulb would suddenly go off. "Oh, never mind," they'd say, "I figured it out."

You could imagine my adult ego feeling annoyed or hurt by this exchange. You don't need me? Why are you wasting my time? My credentials and expertise are useless if all I do is stand there and listen to you walk through your approach to solving the problem. But this thinking is myopic, focused on the wrong thing. What matters in helping another person learn something is what they know, not what you know. Talking out loud as they solve a problem, learners have a chance to transcend the thought paths they've been stuck in and rise to a level of meta-cognition that often leads to breakthroughs.

This can happen even when the other person says nothing. I know professional computer programmers who keep a stuffed animal next to the monitor for exactly this type of conversation, recognizing that the magic is in the reflection. They talk through the problem, watch their own thinking, and find a new and better solution.

Sometimes, the first question leads to more tactical suggestions. Maybe there is a resource, like a book, article, video, or tutorial that the learner is not aware of. Asking what they have tried so far and pointing learners to these additional resources creates the perfect opportunity for learning, without taking away responsibility for the process.

In other instances, the question uncovers a mindset issue. It's easy to be frustrated, devolving into "rage clicking" or the offline equivalents. The idea of clicking the "hint" button might carry a stigma, or even feel like a breach of integrity. When I ask a child what they have tried so far, I often get a glimpse into the messy, human aspect of learning. This question has led to beautiful coaching moments, fostering persistence and developing a growth mindset.

## 2. WHO ELSE HAVE YOU ASKED?

Even for a mindset guru with all the scrappy learning approaches in the world, there are times where we simply don't understand. Maybe the video explanation isn't landing, or we're missing some context, or we're struggling to follow the steps in a tutorial or walkthrough. If a learner is stuck after multiple attempts to figure out a problem on their own, this is the perfect time for the next question: "Who else have you asked?"

The purpose of this question is to break down an imaginary barrier that prevents us from asking for the help we need.

One reason we hesitate to ask for help is that we are conditioned not to. In a traditional classroom, kids are routinely shushed for attempting to communicate with peers, and in some settings it is considered cheating. It's not hard to see why it might feel wrong to seek out knowledge by asking fellow learners.

Another obstacle preventing most of us from asking for help is fear of what they might think of us. No one wants to feel stupid, and it's always easier to keep your head down than to admit you don't know something. Compounding this fear is the norm we just talked about, that each learner should do everything in their power to Figure It Out on their own. Not only do we worry about looking dumb, but we also worry about coming across as lazy or overly dependent.

Despite these concerns, asking for help is an excellent way to learn. It gives you a chance to hear another person talk through their understanding of a topic, which is often different from the reference material or the way an expert might describe it. It provides a chance for the person you ask to deepen their understanding. Most of us have had the realization that learning gets real very quickly when you're trying to explain it to someone else. Beyond the actual transfer of knowledge, asking questions is a reminder of the truth Socrates taught: "The only true wisdom is in knowing that you know nothing."

Clever educators have long understood the value of kids engaging with each other. Many classroom teachers invoke a policy of "three before me," meaning a student with a question should talk to three different classmates before raising their hand for the teacher.

Sometimes, learners feel a little shy about doing this. Part of my role in facilitating Code Club, and later as a microschool guide, was to foster a safe learning environment. That means it is totally fine not to know, asking is judgment-free, and the expectation is that we are all here to help each other. To drive that home, I would occasionally make public service announcements: "Attention everyone. David and I are trying to set up a variable in Scratch and we are a little stuck. Does anyone know how to do this?" When the environment is right, hands shoot into the air, kids come wandering over, new friendships are forged, and I slip quietly away.

A small, flexible learning environment is the perfect place to overcome the stigma and develop the skill of asking good questions. For example, with ten or fewer students from different ages, grade levels, and academic starting points, Prenda microschools provide an excellent training ground for learners. The "mixed age" learning environment creates many opportunities for older students to work with younger ones, driving deep connection and reinforcing the Figure It Out value.

### 3. READY TO FIGURE THIS OUT TOGETHER?

Typically, by the time a learner reads the hint, googles for a bit, watches a tutorial video, experiments with different approaches, and asks others for help, the problem has been solved. But there are moments where this doesn't happen. When I first started Code Club, I was terrified about these moments because I knew deep down that I am not an expert computer programmer. I was sure that a precocious ten-year-old would call me over, stumped by some tricky JavaScript error message, and I would be exposed as a complete fraud. But over time, I lived this exact scenario and others like it. Instead of bringing terror and shame, these moments became powerful coaching opportunities, perfect for installing the habits and mindsets of an empowered learner.

The secret was to drop all pretext of me having all the answers. I needed to disabuse these kids of the idea that the adult in charge was the sole bearer of knowledge, so I stubbornly refused to hand out solutions like candy from a vending machine. This was convenient, because I eventually got plenty of questions for which I did not have answers, and I was able to follow the same pattern.

After a learner has made the effort to solve the problem, asked other kids, and still feels stuck, I come over and ask the final question: "Are you ready to figure this out together?" Then we launch into the learning process all over again. But this time, we do it together.

It happened frequently that this exercise blew the mind of an unsuspecting young person. Sitting there with their hand raised, waiting for me to come over and help them, having completed the gamut of learning steps that I gave them, they fully expected me to solve their problem for them.

They were often surprised by what came next. First, I sat down and told them flat out that I didn't have the answer. Then, I launched into the exact same learning process I had been telling them to do. Google searches, trial and error, asking kids to explain things. Gradually, the inquiring learner moved from bewilderment to impatience.

They think: I could have done this stuff myself, and it would have been faster than bringing this guy over.

I think: *Exactly*.

I want learners to feel fully equipped to find answers and solve the problems in their way. That doesn't mean I leave them alone to fend for themselves. By asking, "Ready to figure this out together?" I am inviting them to be an empowered learner, communicating my deep conviction that they are capable, and supporting them as they build strong learning habits.

You will see this same phenomenon in your learning endeavors, whether giving or receiving the help. It's amazing to find the answer to a specific question; it's even more impactful to watch a learner in action.

These three questions translate the abstract ideas of Figure It Out into a practical approach for everyday learning, applicable to anything you might want to learn in school and much, much more.

1. What have you tried so far?

2. Who else have you asked?

3. Ready to figure this out together?

## One Step at a Time

We've talked about the Figure It Out mindset, hiding places, value in the real world, and tactical questions to apply the value in real life. For the last piece of the puzzle, let's talk about plans. Every goal requires a plan. And when we embark on a big learning goal, the planners among us are inclined to agonize over every aspect of the path ahead.

Plans are good. They get us off the couch and moving forward. They fuel our dreams by making them palpable. They give us guidance for the actions we should take, and help us prioritize between an endless array of possibilities. But there's another thing you should know about plans: they never work out. My favorite quote about this is from the boxer Mike Tyson: "Everybody has a plan, until they get punched in the mouth."

There are dangers in planning, all tied to the inevitably of reality unfolding differently than the plan. One danger is "analysis paralysis." We delude ourselves into believing we can tame the uncertainty, if only our checklist is well thought out. Instead of taking the first step, we fuss over steps nineteen to twenty-three. In reality, whatever you write down for step nineteen will be laughably wrong. Another danger is purely psychological. It feels frustrating when things don't go according to plan, so our tight grip on a false certainty about the future sets us up for disappointment.

Dangers notwithstanding, making a plan is still a good idea. Think of the plan as a clear next step, coupled with a vague sense of where you're headed. You want to have enough of a picture of the future that you have the motivation to take the current step and the next one. Those immediate actions should be crystal clear. But you should expect the long-range plan to change as you collect more information.

This phenomenon is stark in entrepreneurship. In past decades, the conventional wisdom was to spend significant time and energy creating a "business plan," a pile of carefully researched documents about the market trends, financial projects, competitive analysis, intellectual property, etc. Designed by an "old school" type of investor and thrust upon aspiring entrepreneurs who didn't know any better, these plans embodied an illusion of false certainty. Countless hours were wasted arguing about the growth rate assumptions in year three of the spreadsheet model.

Gradually, this paradigm began to change. Thinkers like Steve Blank adapted an old military adage to proclaim, "No plan survives contact with the outside world." Eric Ries introduced the world to the "Lean Startup" approach, where the detailed plan is replaced by carefully prioritized hypotheses to be tested methodically. Professor Clayton Christensen framed every product or service as a "job to be done," simplifying business to the core exchange of value. Marc Andreessen, Netscape creator turned venture capitalist, coined the term "product-market fit." Startup incubator Y Combinator told founders to "make something people want," an approach so simple that it fits on a T-shirt. Together, these shifts in conventional wisdom are a move away from detailed plans accounting for every contingency, toward big visions with very actionable and immediate next steps.

Today, entrepreneurs still think about the future, considering all the strengths, weaknesses, opportunities, and threats. But they also realize that a careful enough analysis of any business plan would likely yield the same conclusion: don't start this business.

There is immeasurable risk, inevitable struggle, and unlikely odds of success. It's always safer to go get a job at an established company. With an audacious vision for how the world could be different, a general direction for how to get there, and a clear first step in mind, entrepreneurs embody the value of Figure It Out.

Thankfully, entrepreneurs aren't the only ones who can Figure It Out. Everyone can apply this type of scrappy resourcefulness, this humble and determined quest for learning, to climb whatever mountain they have chosen. Indeed, it's the only way to do it.

# Figure It Out in Action

WHAT ARE YOU TRYING TO LEARN? WHERE ARE YOU STUCK? IS THERE an area where you'd like to know more? Are you avoiding the work of figuring it out? What hiding places are you using? There's no judgment here. Everyone does it.

When you decide to dive into a wholehearted pursuit of learning, but still find yourself stuck, consider the three questions:

1. What have you tried so far?

2. Who else have you asked?

3. Ready to figure it out together?

Now, what's your next action? If you find yourself needing a detailed plan, that's fine. Get out the notebook, spreadsheet, or Gantt chart, and have a ball. But I'd recommend timeboxing the activity. Give yourself twenty-four hours to come up with the concrete next step in your learning journey, and then start working on it.

# Figure It Out Vignette:

## Starting Prenda

THE LIGHTS WERE DIM AND REDDISH, THE BOOTH SEATS WERE comfortable, and the air was full of curry and spices. My wife Kim and I sat quietly staring at each other across the table, mostly empty dishes pushed to the side. There was one piece of garlic naan in a basket.

This moment was significant, because after years of formal education and a career of stable technology jobs, we were talking seriously about me quitting my job to work full time on the new company I'd started. The mission was simple: to bring code clubs to the world. I had dabbled with entrepreneurship before, but it was always a side hustle. I had never put my livelihood on the line. And the stakes were not low; we had four young children with all the accompanying food and medical expenses, not to mention the mortgage payments.

But somehow, Kim and I felt peaceful and confident. The code club business was bringing in some revenue already, and I felt like I could get more libraries to sign up. And we had some savings in the bank.

Together, we committed to the mountain. Now it was time to continue climbing.

Every day brought new opportunities to Figure It Out. How do you get librarians interested in running afterschool coding programs? Even if you find the librarian, how do you get the library to allocate space and provide computers? How do you find funding for the program inside already constrained budgets? How do you help the library market the program to its patrons and the broader community? How do you help librarians facilitate the code club in a way that allows kids to be engaged owners of their learning?

It took a solid year of figuring out puzzles like these, but the code club business eventually got to a stable place. We had repeat customers, recurring revenue, and now a team of two as I hired Luke Miller to help build the product and deliver the services. Great story, right?

Not exactly.

This was around the same time that I noticed some things based on my experience helping kids learn. I saw the fire that is kindled in the mind when a human makes a choice to learn. I saw how a safe learning environment, a supportive culture, and connections with peers can create a safe haven for budding learners. I talked to homeschoolers, retired teachers, and other adults who were ready and willing to play a major role in helping kids love learning.

As these observations crystalized into the concept of a full curriculum microschool, my Figure It Out list got very long, very fast. What does student-centered learning look like for math and language arts? How would parents respond to the microschool idea? What does the learning guide do? How are they different from a teacher in a traditional classroom? How can we support the guide with remote resources to deliver a complete experience for students? Is there a way I could partner with schools to make the program free to families?

I launched my first microschool around my kitchen table with some partial answers to these questions, and gradually learned how to do a microschool. It was exciting to see how the kids in my microschool were becoming empowered learners. Together, we figured out how to bring math to life through an adapted version of the Three Act Math approach developed by Dan Meyer. We figured out the format for civil and thought-provoking debate, with impassioned arguments about whether school teachers should carry weapons and whether you should, in fact, give a mouse a cookie. We figured out that kids will work hard to improve their writing when they are submitting their work for publication, even if their audience is small. The learning model was showing signs of working, but the learning was just getting started.

Over time, as more and more people joined the Prenda community and opened microschools of their own, I was lucky enough to find a team of talented and passionate people to bring microschools to thousands of students all over the United States. My efforts to Figure It Out expanded to topics like testifying before legislative subcommittees, negotiating partnerships, hiring executives, raising money from investors, speaking at conferences, and many more. It's all learning, and when it's helping empower learners, I can't get enough of it.

# Chapter 4

# Learning > Comfort

HANGZHOU IS THE CAPITAL CITY OF ZHEJIANG PROVINCE IN CHINA. It goes back more than a thousand years, boasting the prosperity of a great location along a narrow bay, with easy access to the East China Sea and navigable inland routes. In the 1960s and early 1970s, when a little boy named Ma Yun was growing up, the Communist Party held tight control over the local government. Ma Yun, his musician parents, and his two siblings were poor compared to their neighbors, and absolutely impoverished by modern US standards.

In 1972, Ma Yun's hometown became a popular tourist destination overnight. Young Ma Yun was intrigued by the visitors and determined to learn from the wealth of experience and knowledge they brought to Hangzhou from all over the world. Every morning, he woke up early and rode his bike to a park, where he offered free tours of the city.

Why was this poor kid making such sacrifices? Why not charge these wealthy tourists? Ma Yun wanted to learn, and he saw this uncomfortable approach as the way to do it. He met a foreign girl who gave him the nickname "Jack," which stuck with him throughout his life.

Learning English as a volunteer for tourists was only the beginning for Jack. He struggled in school, failing his exams twice in elementary school and three times in middle school. He had a hard time getting accepted into a university. He was the only person in a large batch of applicants to get turned down for a job at the new KFC (Kentucky Fried Chicken). Eventually, he made it through college and found a job paying $12 a month as an English teacher.

After years of hustling, Jack had the opportunity to test out the Mosaic web browser on a visit to America in 1995. He was smitten, and quickly became obsessed with bringing the internet to his homeland. He started two technology companies that failed.

Refusing to give up, Jack Ma kept learning, and eventually started Alibaba and Alipay, two companies that have generated enormous value and affected the lives of billions. At one point, Jack was the wealthiest person in China and near the top of the Forbes global list.

When Jack Ma was asked about challenges and rejections, he simply said, "Well, I think we have to get used to it. We're not that good."

Getting used to challenges? Accepting rejection as a necessary part of life? Expecting a bumpy road? I believe entrepreneur Jack Ma embodies our next value: Learning > Comfort.

What does it mean to choose learning over comfort? Why do we write this as an inequality, with a "greater than" sign? And what's wrong with comfort? Isn't that the goal?

To answer these questions and explore the concept, let's imagine you have a goal to build muscles. Maybe you want to show off your toned arms, or improve your rock climbing skills, or take a long hike without being tired. Your friends keep talking about this place called the gym, where people go in weak and come out strong. You purchase a membership, throw on some exercise clothes, walk into the gym, and find your first exercise: the leg press. You set ten-pound weights on each side, lay down on the bench, and use your legs to push the weights into the air. It's easy! You feel awesome, like some sort of superhero! You repeat the motion twenty times and head for the exit. Then you come back the next day and do the same thing. And the next day, and the next, and the next.

As the weeks turn into months and the months turn into years, you might wonder why your muscles are not getting stronger, despite the daily trips to the gym. The reason for your lack of progress is exactly the same reason you enjoy your workouts so much: they are easy! Without the struggle of lifting more weight, you are not building muscle. You're simply going through the motions. It's the resistance that leads to growth.

The same principle applies to learning. When we stay in our comfort zone (and our brains really want to be comfortable), we avoid scary moments like not knowing the answer, failing in front of others, or feeling rejected and alone. We feel safe and secure. But we are not learning.

Now let's return to the gym, reminding ourselves about your big goal of stronger legs. Realizing that you are ready for a bigger challenge, you add some more weight to the leg press. It's harder to push it, but you finish the reps and head home, more tired than you were yesterday. When you come back tomorrow, you stay longer, adding some cardio and other exercises to cross train your different muscle groups. You sweat more. You have sore muscles. Some days, you are not able to complete the set. But gradually, over weeks and months, you notice that you are able to lift more weight. You are getting stronger! And your hard work is paying off; you notice your legs are stronger and more durable for all kinds of other activities you do outside the gym.

In the context of physical activity, this all feels very obvious. Of course I have to struggle in order to get stronger! Of course that process involves some pain. Yet, for some inexplicable reason, most of us expect to grow our brains without any mental discomfort. We might hope for some sort of magical osmosis, where knowledge transfers into our brains without our consciousness. Or maybe we expect to pick up a new skill simply by thinking about it.

Deep down, we all know the truth, even if we don't want to face it: learning requires effort and exertion, and that means we are going to be uncomfortable. Think about the dictionary definition of learning: "To gain knowledge or understanding or skill." Gaining something, the process of acquiring, means that you do not start with it in the first place. In order to *learn*, you first have to *not know*. But we hate not knowing, and so learning is inherently uncomfortable. The discomfort multiplies as we embark on the learning quest: thinking, contemplating, asking, trying, failing, and eventually gaining the knowledge or understanding or skill we were seeking.

If you spend time around hatching chicks, you can watch Learning > Comfort before your very eyes. After being fertilized and laid by their rooster and hen parents, eggs spend about three weeks incubated in a warm, safe place. Sounds comfortable, right? Well, sort of. Inside the shell, the embryonic chick is undergoing all sorts of transformations. Changes in temperature or humidity can be fatal. And with the mortal danger of sticking to the side of the shell, the egg needs to be rotated multiple times per day.

Eventually, the baby chick is ready to enter the world. The chick makes a tiny hole in the shell with its beak, called a pip. You start to hear a constant chirping from within. The egg begins to rock back and forth. A tiny crack or chip appears in the shell. After some more jostling, the crack gets bigger and you can just barely start to see movement inside. More movement, more waiting. The crack finally starts to open up and you can see parts of a downy coat, something frantically wiggling and pushing against its oval prison until it makes its way out of the shell.

Exciting! You just witnessed the miracle of life! Except maybe you didn't witness it, because this process happens slowly over twenty-four hours. You might have dismissed it as boring, or been distracted. Waiting for a chick to hatch can be so excruciating that it becomes dangerous, as well-meaning humans see the baby chick struggling to break out of its shell, feel sympathy, and intervene by "helping" crack the eggshell.

Unfortunately, this intervention almost always results in death for the new chicken. Why? The process of wiggling and pecking and pushing against its shell is exactly what the chick needs in order to build the strength to survive the outside world. Doing the work for the chick deprives it of a growth opportunity, leaving it too weak to walk.

Learning > Comfort may not always be this dramatic, but there are some important points illustrated here:

1. Learning takes time. It's easy to get impatient with the process, especially when we are grappling with new concepts or struggling to master a new skill. But just as the chick takes a long time to push out of its shell, we often need hours, days, weeks, months, or even years to accomplish our learning goals.

2. Learning takes effort. Watching the chick flapping its wings, rocking back and forth, pushing with its tiny sharp beak, there is no question that she is willing to work to achieve her freedom. We also have to exert ourselves, throwing every ounce of our energy into the learning process.

3. Learning is frustrating. You can almost hear the frustration in the constant, high-pitched chirping noises the baby chick makes from the first internal pip to the time it leaves

the shell behind. We might make different sound effects, but we definitely feel the strain of constant effort and repeated setbacks in our learning endeavors.

Thankfully, Learning > Comfort is almost never a life or death scenario for you. Instead of mortal danger, the risk you face exists in your own fears and limiting beliefs. If you can push through those obstacles, you will not only learn, grow, and achieve at levels you never thought possible, but you can become an entirely new person.

The venerable Dr. Seuss captured this concept when he said: "If things start happening, don't worry, don't stew, just go right along and you'll start happening too." It is precisely by adopting this value and choosing learning over comfort that you will "start happening."

## Why Learning Is Uncomfortable

Choosing learning over comfort might seem obvious, but it flies in the face of millions of years of evolutionary biology. It all starts with your brain, one of the greatest energy hogs of all time.

Like every species, humans have to worry about basic survival and reproduction. In our early days, these needs existed in a setting of constant scarcity: not enough food, danger of predators, exposure to the elements. As a result, our brains evolved to conserve energy. Those who could do more with less were rewarded with higher survival rates, more resources, and the ability to pass down genetic material, eventually leading to dense, energy-intensive brains.[16]

But with all that energy intensity came a need for *efficiency*, a need to *conserve* energy. The body burns energy to chase down

---

[16] Ferris Jabr, "How Humans Evolved Supersized Brains," *Quanta Magazine*, November 10, 2015, https://www.quantamagazine.org/how-humans-evolved-supersize-brains-20151110/.

prey, run away from predators, find a cave to hide in, and compete for a mate. On top of that, our energy-hog brains are constantly looking for ways to do these things better, using up even more energy. So even as our brains evolved to our great advantage (think of tools, fire, structures, farming, language), we were presented with an energy crisis. The only solution was to strictly manage our energy budget, amassing more and spending less. For our bodies, this shows up as a preference for a sedentary lifestyle and overeating. For our brains, it is more subtle.

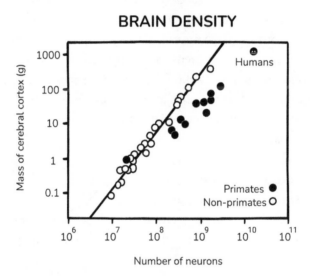

There are numerous ways our brain tries to save energy, all of them presenting a challenge to the Learning > Comfort mindset.

- Automatic versus Reasoning systems. In his book *Thinking, Fast and Slow*, Psychologist Daniel Kahneman explains the interplay of two functional systems in our brains. Yes, we have the capacity to reason and calculate. But we also have an automatic process that handles breathing, walking, and so many of our routine actions.

- Cognitive biases. The "List of Cognitive Biases" page on Wikipedia lists fifteen high-level biases, with many more flavors and variants underneath them. With names as interesting as status quo bias, the hot hand fallacy, and pareidolia, these biases have gained popularity in recent years as evidence that we can't trust our brains.[17] But you can also see these biases as shortcuts our brains use to save energy.

- Herd mentality. Psychologists and sociologists have studied how we are heavily influenced by the thoughts and opinions of those around us. Sticking with the group kept us safe in caveman days, but it doesn't always serve us in the modern world. In one classic experiment, people declared a line was the longest even though it clearly wasn't, after seven actors gave the same (obviously incorrect) answer.[18]

- Heuristics. Defined as "efficient cognitive processes, conscious or unconscious, that ignore part of the information," heuristics are all about saving brain energy.[19] But if we're not careful, they also open us up to all kinds of misconceptions and prevent learning.

Considering the perilous environment and scarce resources faced by our earliest ancestors, it's no surprise that our brains are predisposed to these and other forms of saving energy. Even

---

[17] David McRaney explores this on a blog, podcast, and book under the name "You Are Not So Smart." See: https://youarenotsosmart.com/the-book/.

[18] Saul McLeod, "Solomon Asch – Conformity Experiment," Simply Psychology, last updated December 28, 2018, https://www.simplypsychology.org/asch-conformity.html.

[19] Gerd Gigerenzer and Wolfgang Gaissmaier, "Heuristic Decision Making," *Annual Review of Psychology* 62 (2011): 451–482, https://doi.org/10.1146/annurev-psych-120709-145346.

though our situation differs, modern humans have dense and energy intensive brains, and taking shortcuts is the only way we could actually operate. For example, imagine having to give detailed instructions for each individual muscle in your body, just to walk a few steps. Do you remember when you were learning how to drive a car? Procedures that were once painstakingly tedious become automatic.

There is nothing wrong with using heuristics and shortcuts to give our brains a break. We simply can't be in a fully engaged mode of cognitive effort at all times and in all things. It's impossible!

Instead, we can understand these constant forces to save brain energy. We know our brain is trying to conserve, and as a result, we expect to feel an internal resistance to learning. We experience this as an aversion to discomfort. If you pay attention, you will notice a relentless barrage of instincts, thoughts, impressions, and desires pushing you to seek comfort. Take the easy way, live the unexamined life, follow the path of least resistance. This drive for comfort comes in less obvious packages: don't reinvent the wheel, curiosity killed the cat, stay in your lane, keep your head down. Your brain wants to be comfortable.

## Choosing Learning

Knowing that your brain is forever seeking to conserve energy is only half of the neuroscientific underpinnings of Learning > Comfort. The other thing to understand is that learning happens when you are not comfortable.

In a recent study, Yale neuroscientists set up an experiment for monkeys and monitored the activity in the learning centers of the prefrontal cortex. The monkeys had the choice between two buttons: a red one that delivered a shot of delicious juice 80 percent of the time, and a green one that produced the juice

20 percent of the time. After some trial and error, the monkeys figured out the game and started pushing the red button.

But then the researchers switched the colors, reversing the probability of the sweet juice reward. This was a shock to the system, and it took the monkeys time, effort, and literal brain growth to adapt to the new rules and start pushing the green button. The brain scans were lighting up with direct evidence of learning, connected to this uncertain and volatile situation.

Contrast this with the control group, where the monkeys figured out to push the higher probability button, and nothing changed in the conditions. These monkey brains displayed significantly less learning.

The conclusion of the research? "We only learn when there is uncertainty, and that is a good thing."[20]

How much of our lives are spent seeking safety and stability, like the second group of monkeys? Tell me the formula, and I will follow it. Which university degree will get me the job? What's the next rung in the corporate ladder? We want certainty and stability, and we avoid uncertainty and volatility. In fact, our learning and growth depends on the very uncertainty we try so hard to avoid.

Embracing this concept is at the core of Learning > Comfort. But how does it work in practice?

## The Growth Mindset

It was a pretty standard afternoon in 2014. I was sitting at my laptop, having just completed a task for work, and I was mindlessly and mercilessly throwing emails out to keep my inbox at zero. Suddenly, I noticed a subject line that caught my attention.

---

[20] Bart Massi, Christopher H. Donahue, and Daeyeol Lee, "Volatility Facilitates Value Updating in the Prefrontal Cortex," *Neuron* 99, no. 3 (August 2018): 598–608.E4, https://doi.org/10.1016/j.neuron.2018.06.033.

I reread it and clicked through to a blog post by Sal Khan, titled "Why I'll never tell my son he's smart."[21]

I hadn't met Sal personally at that point (we did connect years later), but I had been an avid user of Khan Academy and respected him as an educational visionary and all-around excellent person. So you can imagine my surprise at seeing this title. *Why would you be so mean to your own flesh and blood? I don't understand!*

Reading the article was my first exposure to the concept of the growth mindset (which we touched upon in Chapter 3). Even though Carol Dweck had been publishing papers on the topic for decades and published a book called *Mindset* in 2007, I was blissfully ignorant. I had no idea what a growth mindset was, or how it could be a powerful tool for an entire generation.

Simply put, a growth mindset is a frame of mind that assumes your brain is capable of learning. In fact, a growth mindset is based on the scientific research that your brain is able to learn anything if you apply enough effort over time. It's the same logic as building muscle through exercise.

In contrast, the fixed mindset assumes that your brain cannot learn, that you either get it or you don't. You can hear a fixed mindset in common expressions like "I am not a math person," "I'm a terrible speller," "I don't have a creative bone in my body," or "computers and I do not get along."

The easiest way to spot a growth mindset is in the way a learner responds to a struggle or challenge. Because learning is uncomfortable, our brains default to a narrative that excuses us from future effort and discomfort. For example, if I take a math test that is easy for me and get a good score on it, I might believe

---

[21] Salman Khan, "The Learning Myth: Why I'll Never Tell My Son He's Smart," *The Blog, HuffPost,* August 19, 2014, https://www.huffpost.com/entry/the-learning-myth -why-ill_b_5691681.

that I am automatically good at math. If I'm good at math, I don't need to work hard at it. So I am unlikely to push myself, tackle new material, think deeply about the concepts I already think I understand, etc. I have a fixed mindset. This is equally true if I get a bad score on the math test and conclude that I am simply not capable of understanding this. If my brain can't learn math, then any attempt to learn it is wasted work leading to unnecessary pain.

Either way, whether I believe I am good at something or not good at something, a fixed mindset encourages me to *not try*. Conveniently, this is the exact same recommendation our energy-conserving brains make as they attempt to protect us from the pain of learning.

In contrast, a growth mindset sees struggle as an opportunity to grow. Instead of avoiding a challenge, shriveling up, or fighting against it, the growth mindset says, *This is great! I am learning something new, and this feeling of discomfort is exactly what I should be feeling.*

You can see how a fixed mindset discourages learning through this simple flow chart.

And you can see how a growth mindset leads to the opposite results, whether the understanding comes easily or not.

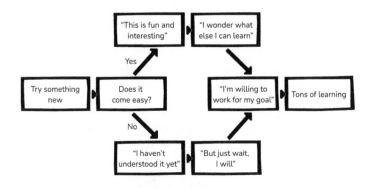

There are many reasons to adopt a growth mindset.

- At the neurological level, Cornell researchers have seen the neural marker that alters the physical state of the brain when it learns.[22] Your brain is literally growing. Of course it hurts!

- It's not just the neurons themselves, but the connections between them too. As described by Daniel Coyle in *The Talent Code*, repeated, focused practice coats neural pathways with an insulator called myelin, speeding up the performance of circuits we use frequently.[23]

---

[22] Ronek Patel, R. Nathan Spreng, and Gary R. Turner, "Functional Brain Changes Following Cognitive and Motor Skills Training: A Quantitative Meta-Analysis," *Neurorehabilitation and Neural Repair* 27, no. 3 (March–April 2013): 187–199, https://doi.org/10.1177/1545968312461718.

[23] Daniel Coyle, *The Talent Code: Greatness Isn't Born. It's Grown. Here's How.* (New York: Bantam Books, 2009).

- Students with a growth mindset are more likely to sign up for advanced courses. This willingness to take risks and embrace challenge will open doors throughout life.[24]

- A growth mindset leads to improved test scores for all types of students. Test scores are an imperfect measure, but this research suggests that a growth mindset can lead to more learning, in and out of the classroom.[25]

- People with a growth mindset have an easier time weathering economic downturns and escaping poverty.[26]

Can you see why adopting a growth mindset is a critical part of becoming an empowered learner? No matter what you want to learn, the first step is to believe that it's possible. It's more than just "feel-good" folklore; the growth mindset gets to the very core of human motivation. Without it, you will probably struggle to get started, and you will certainly give up when things get difficult. And things always get difficult.

But lest you feel like I'm getting preachy, I want to acknowledge that it is nearly impossible to live in a growth mindset all the time. A few years after the concept caught hold in mainstream culture, Carol Dweck wrote an article for Harvard Business Review to clear up a few common

---

[24] "The Evidence: How a Growth Mindset Leads to Higher Achievement," Mindset Kit, video, 3:44, accessed February 7, 2023, https://www.mindsetkit.org/topics/about-growth-mindset/evidence-how-growth-mindset-leads-to-higher-achievement.

[25] Sarah D. Sparks, "Growth Mindset Linked to Higher Test Scores, Student Well-Being in Global Study," *Education Week*, April 9, 2021, https://www.edweek.org/leadership/growth-mindset-linked-to-higher-test-scores-student-well-being-in-global-study/2021/04.

[26] Shan Zhao et al., "Growth Mindset of Socioeconomic Status Boosts Subjective Well-Being: A Longitudinal Study," *Personality and Individual Differences* 168, no. 1 (January 2021): 110301, https://doi.org/10.1016/j.paid.2020.110301; Susana Claro, David Paunesku, and Carol S. Dweck, "Growth Mindset Tempers the Effects of Poverty on Academic Achievement," *PNAS* 113, no. 31 (2016): 8664–8668, https://www.pnas.org/doi/abs/10.1073/pnas.1608207113.

misconceptions that had crept into the popular usage of the term growth mindset.

She said, "Everyone is actually a mixture of fixed and growth mindsets, and that mixture continually evolves with experience. A 'pure' growth mindset doesn't exist, which we have to acknowledge in order to attain the benefits we seek."[27]

## THE POWER OF YET

I had a fixed mindset moment as I was working on this chapter. I was hanging out with a friend who played an incredible piece on the piano. Her fingers were flying across the keys, and the sound of the arpeggios was downright angelic. I let out a respectful whistle, and said, "Never in a million years could I play the piano like that."

Sometimes, we need a pithy axiom or catchy slogan to remind ourselves to rise above our default level. Fortunately, Sesame Street is at the ready.

It's not my number one favorite Sesame Street moment (that honor is reserved for Grover and the Big Hamburger), but I appreciate their music video teaching children about the growth mindset, called "The Power of Yet."

The video starts out with adorable puppets messing up. Bert can't sing the song right. Cookie Monster burns the cookies. Elmo answers a math problem incorrectly. Just in their moment of frustration, singer-songwriter Janelle Monáe walks in with a catchy tune and a troupe of dancers in cool tuxedos. The song is peppy and the video is funny, but the concept is pure power. It's the simple idea that the word "yet" changes a discouraging statement into a hopeful, motivating one.

The power of yet is a practical way to apply a growth mindset. You might not know something…yet. You might not be

---

[27] Carol S. Dweck, "What Having a 'Growth Mindset' Actually Means," *Harvard Business Review*, January 13, 2016, https://hbr.org/2016/01/what-having-a-growth-mindset-actually-means.

good at a skill...yet. Embedded in this word is the optimistic confidence that you can learn what you do not currently know. It just takes commitment, time, and effort.

Carol Dweck accentuates the point in her 2014 TED Talk, pointing to a school in Chicago that doesn't give failing grades, but replaces them with "Not Yet." In the traditional world of Ds and Fs, it is pretty easy to draw the conclusion that you are simply not cut out for this. *Cut out*, as if we were static, unchanging paper dolls or wooden figurines. The fixed mindset is all around us, especially when we don't "fit the mold" of the systems and structures around us.

And with a fixed mindset, we are tempted to do unproductive things as a coping mechanism. Carol Dweck mentions three examples from her original work:

- People with a fixed mindset are more likely to cheat. If I see the system as rigged against me and I feel like there's no productive way forward, I may abandon my morals.[28]

- People with a fixed mindset are more likely to look for someone worse off as a way to feel better about themselves. At least I'm not as dumb as that guy![29]

- People with a fixed mindset are more likely to avoid difficulty. If I believe it is impossible for me to ever do this, then why should I try? I might as well bang my head into a brick wall.[30]

---

[28] See Lisa S. Blackwell, Kali H. Trzesniewski, Carol S. Dweck, "Implicit Theories of Intelligence Predict Achievement across an Adolescent Transition: A Longitudinal Study and an Intervention," *Child Development* 78, no. 1 (2007): 246–263, https://doi.org/10.1111/j.1467-8624.2007.00995.x.

[29] See A. David Nussbaum and Carol S. Dweck, "Defensiveness versus Remediation: Self-Theories and Modes of Self-Esteem Maintenance," *Personality and Social Psychology Bulletin* 34, no. 5 (2008): 599–612, https://doi.org/10.1177/0146167207312960.

[30] See Ying-yi Hong et al., "Implicit Theories, Attributions, and Coping: A Meaning System Approach," *Journal of Personality and Social Psychology* 77, no. 3 (1999): 588–599, https://doi.org/10.1037/0022-3514.77.3.588.

Instead of cheating, gloating, and running away from hardship, what if we simply changed our mind about learning with the power of yet? What if we made a deliberate choice to seek learning, fully expecting to be uncomfortable?

The Prenda team makes a game of it. If someone in a meeting slips into a fixed mindset, pointing out the discouraging reality of limitations, their colleague will add the word "yet" to their sentence. "We are not delivering a good enough experience for our customer...yet." "I can't get the conversion rate for this cohort up...yet." Annoying, for sure, but it's all in good fun and it reminds us that we are all continually learning.

The power of yet is liberating and luxurious in the present because it frees us from the negative self-talk and limiting structures that hold us back. It opens up a world of infinite possibility. What do you want to be? What do you want to know? What do you want to do? These things are available to you. It won't come easily, but you can stick with it if you embrace a growth mindset. Maybe Sesame Street can help.

## PUTTING IT INTO PRACTICE

Now that we have covered the psychology research, made the case for a growth mindset, and sprinkled in some cute puppet characters, let's talk about how to do this in real life. What does a growth mindset look like? How can I shift from a fixed mindset to a growth mindset in the areas that are holding me back?

One of the best things about the growth mindset is that it can change. You can start with a fixed mindset and move to a growth mindset, setting yourself up for learning. So if you believe me about the benefits of a growth mindset, then the question is how to develop one. By incorporating these ideas and practicing them over time, you will find your mindset shifting.

**ADMIT IGNORANCE**

Sometimes you don't know something. It might feel uncomfortable or scary to admit it, but the starting point for literally all learning is a state of not knowing. Accepting ignorance and openly admitting it is an important part of living the growth mindset. It's easier to stomach because you add the word "yet" and fully believe that you can learn it if you try.

The best example I have seen of admitting ignorance is in the librarians running afterschool code clubs. To a person, these good people did not have an extensive background in computer programming. Many of them were women in their sixties who claimed to "barely be able to send an email."

Watching these people interact with the kids at Code Club, I was astonished by their willingness to admit to not knowing. By explaining to the kids that they didn't have the answers, and then modeling the attitudes and behaviors of a learner, they created powerful learning environments.


**WELCOME FEEDBACK**

A growth mindset considers every bit of feedback as an input to the learning process. Instead of feeling defensive or annoyed, you can choose to see feedback as a gift. Reed Hastings, the CEO of Netflix, is famous for wanting feedback. His book *No Rules, Rules* includes stories where Reed received hard feedback, the kind that would terrify most people, and instead of punishing the person, he thanked them.

Receiving feedback does not mean you agree with it, or that you are obligated to change anything. Reed Hastings certainly doesn't always act on every bit of feedback, but he sincerely appreciates it, considers it, and uses it as a tool to support his personal learning and growth.

## DROP PERFECTIONISM

Have you heard the expression "perfect is the enemy of the good?" Most of us have felt the painful discomfort of learning something new. We want to be better than we are, and when we make the inevitable and frequent mistakes of the early learning process, we are tempted to give up or stick with what we know.

The best advice in these situations is to do the opposite. Accept the mistakes and keep going forward. I saw this in an animation class I took with my kids. I was surprised to see how carelessly the professional illustrator laid down layer upon layer of pencil. Many of them went in the wrong direction, and he never worried or erased anything, just constantly revised and added to his illustration.

This concept shows up in many areas. Consider the budding pianist who may want to restart her piece from the beginning after missing one note, but her teacher encourages her to continue the piece as if nothing had gone wrong. The advice applies in writing as well; getting a first draft down on paper is always better than staring at a blank page and dreaming of perfect prose. To reinforce the idea of a "crappy first draft" in a comical but terrifying way, Manuel Ebert created "The Most Dangerous Writing App," where the text on your page starts to fade out and eventually disappears forever if you stop writing. Better to write something imperfect than to write nothing at all.

One young learner in a Prenda microschool had an especially strong perfectionist streak. She was working in a math tool that told her when she messed up, and the frequent reminders that she hadn't yet mastered the particular topic was pushing her to a breaking point. She yelled at the computer, claiming it was wrong. In tears, she told her learning guide, Bekah, that she simply couldn't go on. This guide, full of love and patience and wisdom, sat down with the student and listened until she understood what was happening. She asked the girl to repeat after her: "I made a mistake and that's okay." After resisting at first, then mumbling in acquiescence, the child finally repeated the phrase. Bekah said it with her. They repeated it again and again until the words sunk in. Both the adult and child were crying now, as the powerful truth emerged. You are valuable and capable. You're learning, and mistakes are part of the process. You'll get this eventually. And sure enough, she did.

## EMBRACE THE SUCK

United States Navy Seals have a tongue-in-cheek expression that simultaneously acknowledges the frequent difficulties and challenges they face and thumbs their noses at it: "embrace the suck." Underneath this somewhat cynical phrase is a sense of humor and even optimism. Sure, the terrain is difficult, and you're sleep deprived, and there are people trying to kill you. That's all part of the job, along with so much more. This attitude—not only enduring the hard times but embracing them—builds an almost superhuman ability to persist. It's a strong enhancer of a growth mindset.

Admiral Jim Stockdale was the highest-ranking US serviceman captured and imprisoned in the Hanoi Hilton during the Vietnam War. Over eight years of harsh treatment, heavy deprivation, and frequent torture, he learned firsthand about embracing the suck. As popularized by Jim Collins, the "Stockdale Paradox" combines a willingness to confront the brutal facts about your situation with the unwavering belief that things will get better.[31] This is exactly what a growth mindset is all about.

There is strong evidence that you can change your mindset. My hope is that you will choose a growth mindset, and that these tips will help you to put it into practice.

---

[31] Jim Collins, "The Stockdale Paradox," JimCollins.com, accessed February 7, 2023, https://www.jimcollins.com/concepts/Stockdale-Concept.html.

## The Learning Frontier

Choosing learning over comfort means you are never satisfied with work that doesn't challenge and stretch you. You want to grow, and you know that happens at the edges of your understanding: your learning frontier.

I am an amateur chess player. Years ago, I signed up for chess.com, and since then I have played chess online against strangers from all over the world. The software matches me with people my same skill level, so if you look at my stats, you'll see I win and lose with equal frequency. (My actual all-time record is 673 wins, 644 losses, and 84 draws.) I'm at my learning frontier, winning a lot and losing a lot. This can be frustrating, since I'd rather win all the time, but I like it because I am getting better. Sure, I could play beginners and feel good about winning, but I wouldn't be learning. And maybe I could learn more if I only played masters and lost every match, but that would feel pretty demoralizing and I might quit.

The learning frontier is like the happy medium from the Goldilocks story: not too hard, not too easy, just right for productive learning. It's where you want to be.

Researchers in the education field refer to the learning frontier as the "zone of proximal development" (ZPD). By definition, the ZPD describes an area you don't currently understand, but that is next to, or proximal to, the knowledge you've already acquired.

For example, suppose you had learned the concept of fractions and started adding fractions with the same denominator, like $2/7 + 3/7$. Now you get a problem that looks similar, but the fractions have different denominators: $1/2 + 1/4$. What do you do?

This is the zone of proximal development. With help, you can learn how to express the equivalent version of a fraction with a different denominator: $1/2$ is the same as $2/4$. Amazing! Now I can do what I already know how to do: add the fractions with the same denominator.

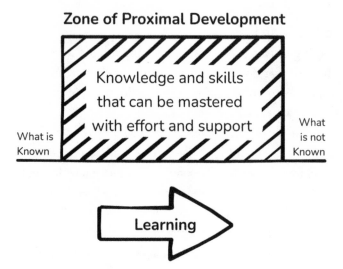

**Zone of Proximal Development**

Knowledge and skills that can be mastered with effort and support

What is Known

What is not Known

Learning

Learning > Comfort means constantly looking for your ZPD. You want to be right at the edge, not because it is comfortable, but because that is where the learning happens. Where is your learning frontier? How can you take the next step, just outside the place you know, to expand your skills and knowledge?

Hopefully, this work will lead you in the direction of the mountain you chose to climb in Daring Greatly. It will certainly require you to Figure It Out. And as we'll see in the next two chapters, it will almost certainly include other people.

# Learning > Comfort in Action

IS THERE A TOPIC AT YOUR LEARNING FRONTIER THAT YOU FIND yourself avoiding? Do you catch yourself believing a narrative that you "aren't built for this," or otherwise reinforcing a fixed mindset? Are you resisting the uncomfortable parts of learning, like receiving feedback, feeling stupid, or having to grind through?

Try this simple checklist to improve your growth mindset and keep learning, even when it's not comfortable.

- Remind yourself of your big goal. Write it down or review what you already wrote down.

- Make a list of the skills or knowledge you need to achieve your goal.

- Reading through your list, highlight in one color everything that seems scary or uncomfortable.

- Highlight in a different color everything that feels "proximal" to what you already know.

- Pick one thing from your list that has both color highlights and initiate the Figure It Out sequence.

- Expect it to be hard, remembering that your brain is trying to conserve energy.

# Learning > Comfort Vignette:

## Kim's Story

THROUGH ALL THE YEARS OF CODE CLUB AND OVER THE FIRST THREE
semesters of Prenda microschools, my wife, Kim, had a front row
seat. A microschool was meeting every day in her house! Her kids
were experiencing school in a pretty different way.

Kim was always supportive as a spouse, but was not enthralled
with the idea in those early days. There were children everywhere,
which meant noise, messes, and a husband that was often depleted
and unavailable.

But the concerns ran deeper than minor inconveniences. She
could tell that the kids enjoyed being there, but she wondered if
this high-energy, sometimes chaotic setting could really be a place
of learning. Like all of us, Kim's experience in school was mostly
about sitting quietly at a desk and filling out worksheets. Now she
was seeing a group of kids who set their own learning goals, designed
creative projects, and collaborated all the time. Kim's college degree
was in elementary education, where she was schooled in the status
quo. The microschool certainly looked different.

For example, if children have ownership, will they really learn?
Kim occasionally found a student who was choosing not to work on
goals. Even in cases where the student had already completed all

the learning goals for the day, the idea of a student "off task" was unsettling. Another question on her mind was the role I played as a guide, not a teacher. Don't they need an adult making sure all the knowledge gets into their heads? What about classroom management? It seemed like exhausting work, and while she was supportive of me doing it, Kim had zero interest in getting more involved.

But as time went on, Kim got to know the children in my microschool. She noticed the changes in them, often hearing from their parents (many of whom were personal friends) about the engagement and enthusiasm their kids were bringing not just to academics, but to other areas of life. She heard the questions, too, like "Shouldn't school hurt a little?" but she started to see the disconnect between the traditional structure and real, empowered learning.

One day, Kim shocked me by saying she wanted to be a learning guide. After three semesters as a guide myself, I was getting too busy with supporting others and building a company. Our youngest daughter, Maisy, was begging to join a microschool, but it didn't seem like it would work out.

That's when Kim realized she could make Maisy's dream come true, while putting to use her education background and her natural affinity for loving children, by creating a microschool for Maisy and her friends. It wasn't an easy decision. She knew all too well that the work was emotionally and physically exhausting. She was still unconvinced on some aspects of the educational philosophy. She had just recently sent our youngest to school, meaning her grueling work as a stay-at-home mom could have gotten a little easier.

But despite the allure of a quiet home and a comfortable life, Kim felt drawn to do this. I was nervous. Was she feeling pressure from me? On the inevitable hard days, would she feel resentment?

She assured me that this was completely her decision. And even though it was a surprise to both of us, she felt confident that it was the right move, not just for ten lucky K–2 children, but for her personal growth as well.

Kim dove into that school year with a commitment to Learning > Comfort. And while she certainly experienced a lot of discomfort, she also felt herself expanding and changing as she made a meaningful difference in the lives of some pretty special kids.

# Chapter 5

# Start with Heart

THE OKLAHOMA AFTERNOON WAS MUGGY AND QUIET AS THE CAR carrying fourteen-year-old Josh Shipp pulled up to the house. He looked through the car window, filled with fear, anger, and distrust as he prepared to meet another set of complete strangers. He was expected to consider these people his new parents. This was not Josh's first stop in the foster system, and he had the psychological scars to prove it. He was incapable of hope or trust, and as he stared at the man waiting for him on the porch, all he could think about was how he could harass this man about his weight. His goal was to get kicked out of yet another foster home.

Looking at his life history, it's easy to understand Josh's state of mind. He had been abandoned by his parents at a very early age. He had been raped by another foster kid. He had been mercilessly bullied, and even survived an attempted suicide. Over time, he came to believe that he could trust no one, and this mistrust manifested in a brash, rude, ungrateful manner that led the adults in his life to believe that he was simply a bad kid.

As Josh tells the story, he spent several years living with this new foster parent, Rodney. He was constantly pushing and poking and prodding, but he never succeeded in getting Rodney to kick him out.

One night, Rodney got a call from Josh, who was locked up at the police station. He had taken a car without permission, without a driver's license or car insurance, and had been pulled over driving well above the speed limit. Rodney consented to come to the station and bail Josh out (after letting him spend the night in jail).

You can imagine the awkwardness of the ensuing conversation. But instead of losing his cool and sending Josh packing, Rodney had a different response, one that cut through the facts of the arrest, bad behavior, and attitude. This moment would change Josh's life. Rodney looked into his eyes and said, "Son, you can keep causing problems. You can keep trying to mess up. You can keep pushing us away. You can keep trying to get us to kick you out of here, but you've got to get it through your thick head, son: *We don't see you as a problem*, we see you as an opportunity."

For the first time in his life, Josh experienced the feeling of being seen, not as a problem or an obstacle, but as a real person with real potential. He was never the same. Josh went on to share his experience and perspective with millions through his writing and speaking. After pointing out his own dangerous proximity to becoming a negative statistic, Josh asserts: "Every kid is ONE caring adult away from being a success story."[32]

Think about the level of true esteem, respect, unfailing positive regard, and action-oriented love that Rodney displayed for Josh. It wasn't unicorns and fairy dust. It wasn't an oblivious denial of reality. It wasn't really even a single dramatic moment. Rodney made a decision that he would see Josh in a particular way, and he stuck to that commitment despite countless reasons to renege.

Early in the Prenda journey, our team of ten sat down in a classroom in the unremarkable basement of a city-owned

---

[32] Josh Shipp, "About," JoshShip.com, accessed February 7, 2023, https://joshshipp.com/about/.

building, with the goal of writing down our core values. We had just articulated our mission in two words: empower learners. Now it was time to explore the behaviors and beliefs that would help our new company empower learners at a scale the world had never seen.

We reflected on our personal experiences with caring adults in our lives. We thought about the role we played as parents to our own children, volunteers in our communities and neighborhoods. We considered the role of formal and informal educators who have formed genuine connections and motivated and inspired empowered learning.

Pulling from the experience I had recently completed as the learning guide for a group of kids in my house, and extrapolating forward to imagine millions of children thriving within the microschool format, one thing became crystal clear. Children need the safety and assurance of an adult they can trust. It's a critical prerequisite. Without a caring adult that makes it real through genuine connection, pedagogy and philosophy fall empty and flat. Teddy Roosevelt had it right: "People don't care how much you know until they know how much you care." With this insight, we realized we needed to design around caring adults in a deliberate way. It had to be at the core.

We named the value "Start with Heart."

Start, because this is a principle of action, requiring a deliberate effort in the way we see others and how we interact with them. Heart, because this is not a tactic or calculation. The only way this value works is through authentic caring for others.

As we've grown, I have had the honor of meeting hundreds of learning guides. Each one brings a unique set of gifts, talents, interests, and tastes. Some are loud; others are quiet. Some love literature; others prefer math. Some are huggers; others prize the personal space. Underneath all of this in the thoughts and souls of these amazing people is the ability to see children as human beings, worthy of respect and love because of the inherent value that all human beings have. They see opportunity and potential in each child, even on days when the child is not living up to it or even deliberately making a stink. They Start with Heart.

Up to this point in the book, we have discussed attributes of empowered learners that can be done independently. In theory, you can Dare Greatly, Figure It Out, and choose Learning > Comfort if you are the only living soul on the planet. But you are not the only living soul on the planet, and the reality is that interactions with other people are an incredible source and support for learning. Empowered learners learn with and from other humans.

## Why Start with Heart

If you've interacted with another person for a prolonged period at any point in your life, you probably know that it's hard to consistently love and respect them. People say and do things we don't like. Sometimes they are gross. They can be obstinate or obsequious. It's always easier to write them off, ignore them, and avoid deep and meaningful connections. But empowered learners make the decision to Start with Heart anyway. Why?

### CONNECTEDNESS IS MANDATORY

One reason to Start with Heart is that you can't actually avoid other humans. Unless you're on a survivalist TV show, dropped in the middle of nowhere, your life isn't set up for rugged individualism.

Somewhere around the turn of the sixteenth century, English poet John Donne observed that "no man is an island." We live in connection with every other person on the planet. Comparing the human race to a continental land mass, Donne points out that each person matters, and that the loss of one is felt by all of us. Even for the most prolific introverts, being human means an inherent connectedness to the lives of many other people. You don't get to choose to be an "island, entire of itself." Ruling out that possibility and simply acknowledging the inherent connectedness of your life to countless others is a first step, but it doesn't mean you will automatically Start with Heart. Connectedness is mandatory, but connection requires a conscious choice and consistent effort. It starts with how you view the people around you.

If you choose to Dare Greatly, it is not only necessary to interface with others but also wise. Your experience will teach you that learning is not the great feat of solo heroics as it's sometimes presented in our mythology. Learning is a collective act where we improve with and through connections to other people. This wisdom has been captured in the old proverb from the Seneca people from the Great Lakes region of North America: "He who would do great things should not attempt them all alone."

## SO MUCH TO LEARN

The people all around you are filled with perspectives, information, opinions, and skills that are different from you. Each one will react to the same situation in a different way. They have probably read different books and articles, listened to different podcasts, made different life choices. They have been to different places and done different things. Even among members of the same neighborhood or family, humans are different in exciting and interesting ways. There is a nearly infinite body of potential learning to be found by simply seeking to understand the human beings in your path.

You might think you understand someone already and have nothing to learn from them. Maybe you have categorized them in your mind as a member of a group whose beliefs and attitudes you fully understand. Perhaps you have spent so much time together that you assume you can predict their every move. But you're almost certainly wrong. Bill Nye the Science Guy knows a lot more than most of us, and he says, "Everyone you will ever meet knows something you don't."

Researcher Todd Rose and his team at Populace ran an experiment to test how well we understand the people around us. As documented in the book *Collective Illusions*, the researchers asked more than 5,000 people to define a successful life. Almost all of them (97 percent) chose a description of success based on following one's interests and talents. But when asked what they thought other people would choose, 92 percent of the respondents chose the other option, that success is defined as being rich, famous, or powerful.[33] Right in these survey results, we can see that most of us are off in our assessment of others, especially when it comes to the inward and interesting questions.

I've experienced this over and over again, thinking I have someone figured out, only to discover that the truth is much more nuanced and sometimes shockingly different than I had assumed. Even up close—my wife and I continue to learn about each other after twenty years of marriage.

Because we miscalculate the intentions of others, it's all too easy to turn life into a competition. But instead of a zero-sum game where I can only win if you lose and vice versa, learning is limitless. Choosing to view our interactions as collaborative and open, choosing to see others as teammates rather than competitors, means we escape the confines of threatening competition and can genuinely give and receive help from each other.

One of my favorite stories about this comes courtesy of writer Ryan Holiday, in a domain where it seems impossible to think in anything other than zero-sum terms: boxing. In

---

[33] Todd Rose, *Collective Illusions: Conformity, Complicity and the Science of Why We Make Bad Decisions* (New York: Hachette Books, 2022).

1956, Floyd Patterson knocked out Archie Moore to become the heavyweight boxing champion of the world. You can imagine how Archie might feel about Floyd, after being punched in the face repeatedly and losing his status as the best in the world in a sport where there is little historical precedent for getting back on top.

Just a few years later, Floyd Patterson experienced the pain himself. He lost the title in a match where he made costly mistakes. He went home and moped, struggling with the sensation of losing. Then one day, Floyd received a letter from Archie Moore, who knew exactly what it feels like to get knocked out and lose the title. Moore's letter basically tells Floyd to quit the pity party, get up, and get to work: "If you concentrate on your jab and move around this guy, you can be the first one to regain the crown. You can do it. Your friend, Archie Moore."[34]

Even in a sport where winning is defined by hurting an opponent so much they can't stand up, this story shows the power of framing learning as collective and not competitive.

## CONNECTION FEELS GOOD

Intuitively, we understand that feeling close with others is good for us. When we are honest, who doesn't appreciate the feeling of unity and meaning that comes from a genuine connection with another person? Research in recent years has validated this. A group at the Stanford Medical School ties greater social connection to lower levels of stress and anxiety.[35] Healthy connections can even extend your lifespan!

---

[34] Ryan Holiday, *Discipline Is Destiny: The Power of Self-Control* (London: Profile Books, 2022), 110–111.

[35] Emma Seppala, "Connectedness & Health: The Science of Social Connection," The Center for Compassion and Altruism Research and Education, Stanford Medicine, May 8, 2014, http://ccare.stanford.edu/uncategorized/connectedness-health-the-science-of-social-connection-infographic/.

Think about the last time you laughed with a friend. Not a polite chuckle or a laugh of cynical derision, but a hearty, all-out, genuine bout of laughing. Like the kind that lasts for minutes, and you're not even sure what's funny, and you're wiping tears from your eyes, and way later in the conversation a simple word or even a look reminds everyone and you're back to uncontrollable laughter. Scientists are just starting to understand why, but laughing together with another person strengthens social relationships and unlocks the benefits of genuine connection.[36]

It doesn't have to be laugh-out-loud funny to be connecting. Any shared experience ties people together. This is part of why we go to dinner together, see movies together, play sports together, and work together. Especially in the hard times, knowing we have the companionship and support of a trusted person can help us bear the load. Connection might be more than a "nice to have," but an important part of surviving and thriving.

## OUR ONLY HOPE

Connecting with others is more than just bumping into people, enjoying them, and learning from them. It may be a matter of life and death. According to the Centers for Disease Control, social isolation increases the risk of premature death to a level comparable to smoking and obesity.[37]

Not only do we need connection for our individual health and well-being, but we need each other to overcome the problems and challenges that we face as a species. Climate change, the threat of nuclear war, social unrest around race and class,

---

[36] Lawrence Robinson, Melinda Smith, and Jeanne Segal, "Laughter Is the Best Medicine," HelpGuide.org, last updated December 5, 2022, https://www.helpguide.org/articles/mental-health/laughter-is-the-best-medicine.htm.

[37] "Loneliness and Social Isolation Linked to Serious Health Conditions," Centers for Disease Control and Prevention, last reviewed April 29, 2021, https://www.cdc.gov/aging/publications/features/lonely-older-adults.html.

global pandemics, economic meltdown—the list goes on and on. These problems are too big for one person to solve alone; they require coordination across hundreds and thousands and millions of empowered learners.

Learning together may be our only hope to elevate our species to the next level. This is more than just peaceful coexistence, where we occupy the same spaces and sit politely while we inwardly despise and abhor the people around us. It's an active posture of learning with and from other people, leading to high levels of collaboration, creativity, collective problem solving, and overall thriving. It all starts with the way we see each other.

## Infinite Value and Unlimited Potential

Starting with Heart is deep and inward and personal. Your behavior can reveal hints and clues, but the extent to which you are living this value can only be truly known by you. The key is a fearless examination of your internal narrative about others. When you see another human, what do you see? How do you view the people in your life, whether close family members, casual acquaintances, or perfect strangers? Are they annoying obstacles you must successfully navigate? Are they pawns in your scheme of world domination? Are they relentlessly blocking any attempt you make at peace and happiness?

To Start with Heart is to believe two simple things about the people around you:

### 1. THEY HAVE INFINITE VALUE

The worth of a person is not something they have to earn or prove. It's automatic. Each of us has inherent value that transcends our daily struggles and all normal expectations. Seeing this infinite worth in other people frees us from the prejudices and petty squabbles that block connection. It can feel like a radical position, as author Bob Goff hints: "No one expects us to love them flawlessly, but we can love them fearlessly, furiously, and unreasonably."[38]

## 2. THEY HAVE UNLIMITED POTENTIAL

The human capacity for learning and growth is one of those things we consistently underestimate. Combine this with very long time horizons, and the potential in humans is practically limitless. According to Muhammad Yunus, the Bangladeshi entrepreneur and Nobel Peace Prize winner who pioneered microloans, "All human beings have unlimited potential, unlimited capacity, unlimited creative energy."[39]

To better understand these two core beliefs, think about a newborn baby. Brand new to the world, babies are completely helpless. They need us for literally everything. They disrupt our sleep and require our constant sacrifice. They create disgusting smells and substances. They cry and burble and drool, and generally don't add anything of interest to the conversation. And yet we just stare at them and smile. We expect nothing from them, and we are thrilled to just be in their presence. Why?

It's easy to see infinite value in a brand new baby. It's natural, miraculous, automatic. Newborn humans are simply valuable. We want to hold them, protect them, and we expect nothing in return. Holding my children in my arms in the first minutes after their birth, it would have been hard to convince me that I could ever feel anything but deep, permanent love for them.

---

[38] Bob Goff, *Everybody Always: Becoming Love in a World Full of Setbacks and Difficult People* (Nashville: Nelson Books, 2018).

[39] Piotr Dutkiewicz, "Muhammad Yunus with Piotr Dutkiewicz," in *22 Ideas to Fix the World: Conversations with the World's Foremost Thinkers*, eds. Piotr Dutkiewicz and Richard Sakwa (New York: New York University Press, 2013), 3.

Connected to this sense of reverence and awe, holding a new baby fills us with wonder and excitement. Everything is possible for this newly-arrived human. It's a blank book waiting to be written. And even though I know life will include hardship and challenges, I can see that the possibilities extend in so many directions as to be endless. It's sheer, unlimited potential.

These two truths—that humans have infinite value and unlimited potential—are true for everyone on the planet. Believing these things does not mean life is easy, and it's not a delusional denial of the hard realities around us. I learned this firsthand when, through a connection in my church community, I found myself visiting a friend in the hospital who had just delivered a newborn baby. This friend—the baby's mother—had a difficult past scarred by abuse, poverty, and addiction. It came out while she was in the hospital that she was using methamphetamines throughout the pregnancy, resulting in a host of physical challenges for the baby and suggesting the likelihood of a very difficult road ahead. My heart broke for this brand new child.

As I held the baby in my arms, I pondered about my beliefs. Does this human have infinite value? It was obvious to see that the answer was yes! Innocent, freshly arrived, perfectly helpless, I was looking at a person that matters just as much as me or you or anyone else. I felt an urge to do everything I could to help this child. Then I asked the second question: does this baby have unlimited potential? I knew the medical challenges he was facing and the complicated home environment where he would grow up. He was given a starting point in life that was harder than most. Could I honestly say that his potential was unlimited? Staring into that newborn's face, I recognized something profound: this baby, like all of us, enters the world completely innocent. He will face challenges that he has no control over, but they do not define him or limit his potential. He deserves to be loved and supported as he figures out who he is and learns to live his life, which could surprise all of us.

Start with Heart is the deliberate attempt to preserve the sense of reverence, respect, and wonder that we automatically feel for babies, and extend this view to every human being. It's deliberate because, as we all know, this perspective does not come naturally when we encounter humans in their larger forms. It's an attempt because we will not get this right the first or second or ten thousandth time. The only way to successfully adopt and apply the core beliefs of Start with Heart is to keep trying.

Eventually, we will find ourselves playing a part in the story of another human, and there is nothing better.

## Be a Helper

We've already talked about the Hero's Journey in Chapter 2, Dare Greatly. As you remember, this is a structure for thinking about the adventure of a protagonist called to leave behind the ordinary world, embark on a quest, and emerge with greater wisdom and confidence. The Hero's Journey is all about learning.

As exciting as it is to be the hero of your very own Hero's Journey (and we all are), it is an even greater sensation to play a role in the journey of another. Looking closely at the archetype, the hero never traverses their path alone. Important support roles with names like Herald, Ally, and Mentor help at key points along the way. When we Start with Heart, we have the unique privilege of playing a helping role for another person in their journey.

In other words, everyone is a hero (of their own journey) and a helper (of someone else's). This is what it means to live in a connected, interdependent world, and be the best version of ourselves.

As a child, I attended a public elementary school in a middle class neighborhood in the suburbs of Phoenix, Arizona. I was a quiet student whose main goal was to avoid any trouble, and so most of my teachers appreciated that I didn't require a lot of time.

In third grade, when I landed in the classroom of Miss Pew, I immediately realized something was different. Somehow, without her actually saying it or really doing anything drastically different, the kids in Miss Pew's class knew that she believed in us. She challenged us to memorize inspirational quotes. She laughed and smiled with us. She took us to the school library and encouraged our various interests.

Miss Pew invited us to participate in the Young Authors program, where kids like me could have the experience of writing and publishing our very own book. I thought this was basically the coolest thing, so I eagerly signed up. Even though I was eight years old, I believed I could write something that people would want to read. At least Miss Pew would want to read it, anyway.

With support from Miss Pew, I set about writing my book. This wasn't an assignment to just "phone it in." There was no rubric or grade or requirement. I wanted it to be great! I worked hard imagining the characters, the setting, and the plot. I wrote multiple drafts. I iterated on grammar and syntax. I used my finest penmanship and I agonized over each illustration.

After months of work, I finished my novella. I don't remember what the story was about, but I can remember the pride I felt for the fabric-covered book, my own title and cover design, and my name proudly staring back at me. The best part was that the school library added a checkout card on the inside cover so that other kids could borrow my book and read it. I felt like a hero. It wasn't until years later that I realized the important mentorship role Miss Pew played in my hero's journey.

Mentors and allies and friends show up in almost every success story. Think of the ground crew for the space shuttle missions, or the deputy of the military leader, or the sports coach. My favorite Start with Heart examples come in the context of learning.

Let's take Andrew Carnegie, for example. Arriving in America as a destitute immigrant in 1848, his family was forced to work hard for basic survival. Andrew was carrying part of the load, working in a factory from age thirteen. There was no time for school. Enter John Anderson, a colonel in the army and a wealthy gentleman in the town. Colonel Anderson owned a private library of more than 400 books. Realizing that those books may do some good, he opened up his collection to working boys in the neighborhood every Saturday. Young Andrew Carnegie was there week after week, borrowing stacks of books and reading them all. Years later, as the wealthiest person on the planet, Carnegie felt so indebted to Colonel Anderson that he committed to pay it forward, building public libraries all over the world so that poor children like himself could experience the life-changing benefits of self-education. John Anderson was a helper in Carnegie's hero story, and Carnegie used his success to be a helper in the hero stories of countless others.

More recently, Richard Williams played a helper role in the heroes' journeys of his tennis superstar daughters, Venus and Serena. Despite challenges in his own life and living in a place not known for tennis (the Compton neighborhood in Los Angeles), Richard saw potential in his two daughters. He believed that they could be number one in the world, meticulously planned for how that would happen, and expected hard work and discipline. Combined with their natural talent, strong family support, and lots and lots of practice, it was a recipe for success.

You can play the role of helper, mentor, and ally in the hero's journey of the people around you. It is one of the most fulfilling and worthwhile things you can do. And in return, the people around you can play these roles in your hero's journey.

Regardless of your age and occupation, and independent of which mountain you are climbing, your empowered learner journey will be more fun and more successful if you look for ways to help others and accept help from them. Let's look at a few examples.

## AT HOME

Personal relationships, like the ones we form with romantic partners, siblings, parents, and children, can bring enormous joy and satisfaction to life. But they can also be our biggest source of pain and suffering.

While it's tempting to look at our relationships in terms of what we expect from others, we can reframe the problems and regain the locus of control by working on how we choose to see others. There is an emerging movement of people trying to do just that: find freedom in relationships by rewriting their narratives about the people around them. Life coaches share these approaches with thousands of individuals through podcasting and one on one coaching. Like coaches of all types, they are often holding up a mirror to help people see the habits and practices that are holding them back. When their clients can clearly see how their perceptions and narratives about their loved ones are not serving them well, they are ready to see other people in a new and liberating way.

## AT SCHOOL

Since the early days of education in America, students have felt the pressure of competition. Only the elite few get into the best schools, your work and knowledge are constantly being evaluated, and you are often ranked in comparison to other students. But thinking of education as a competition can be soul-crushing, especially if you feel like your identity is tied to the outcome.

I saw both sides of this coin as a graduate student at the Massachusetts Institute of Technology. The student body at MIT is an impressive group, bringing a high aptitude for science and engineering and a sturdy track record of academic achievements. Tuition is high, the coursework is demanding, and all kinds of career trajectories are in play.

With that backstory, you might expect to see people feeling the pressure. This certainly happens; MIT students are used to being the top of their class, but they suddenly feel below average when they arrive on campus. The hit to identity and self-worth can be devastating, and in tragic cases can lead to extreme depression and suicide.

At the same time, I was amazed to see such a strong spirit of collaboration and camaraderie among the students. On any given night in the public computer labs, you could find groups of undergrads commiserating about a challenging topic and helping each other through the problem sets. For these students, seeing other students as teammates rather than competitors not only helped them master the material, but created lasting friendships.

Learning together, in a collaborative and positive way, is more fun and more effective.

## AT WORK

There was a time in Corporate America where the norm was to unapologetically climb ladders, positioning yourself as the strongest candidate for the promotion and even undercutting other people that you see as competitors.

But things have changed, and most successful organizations today reject that type of behavior. Instead of playing office politics, looking out for number one, and destroying the competition, top performers in the business world today see their work as a team sport.

Think of the age-old business practice of networking. In the past, you might picture people in suits exchanging business cards and calculating how they can maximize their results by way of another person. Today's business leaders feel inauthentic and even dirty about that approach, instead opting for genuine connection. Transactional networking has been replaced by something that feels much closer to seeing human beings and trying to help them. Consider the four tips on networking from a recent article in the *Harvard Business Review*: focus on learning, identify common interests, think broadly about what you can give, and find a higher purpose.[40] Framing our work relationships around helping others is good for our business success, but the real reason to Start with Heart is that it honors the value and potential of the humans all around us.

## AT PLAY

Americans have more free time than ever before, and that means a seemingly endless array of possible hobbies and interests to pursue. In contrast to other domains, we all seem to understand that our recreational pursuits are better and more rewarding with friends. I know people who meet every Saturday to tackle a new hiking trail. My brother-in-law regularly meets with friends on mountain biking expeditions. One of my friends hosts a meetup for singles in their fifties and sixties who enjoy cooking.

Scott Heiferman wanted to help people form their own groups, and so he co-founded Meetup.com. His advice is to "find your conspirators, folks who share a passion with you."[41]

---

[40] Francesca Gino, Maryam Kouchaki, and Tiziana Casciaro, "Learn to Love Networking," *Harvard Business Review*, May 2016, https://hbr.org/2016/05/learn-to-love-networking.

[41] Scott Heiferman, "How Did I Get Here?" Bloomberg, 2015, https://www.bloomberg.com/graphics/2015-how-did-i-get-here/scott-heiferman.html.

When we come together around a common interest, it can be easy to seek out chances to help others. It's just what groups do.

There are opportunities all around you to practice Starting with Heart. Whether at home, at school, at work, or at play, you can decide to be the helper in someone else's story. As you do, you will find personal satisfaction and build lasting connections.

## Frameworks for Starting with Heart

Seeing the infinite value and unlimited potential in others is not easy. How do you put this value into practice? What will you do when your mindset starts to slip? Fortunately, I'm not the first one to suggest living life this way. In fact, the ideas of truly seeing and accepting other people and contributing to others are central in numerous worldviews and spiritual and religious traditions. In this section, I will share two frameworks I have found particularly helpful when Starting with Heart.

### LOVING WHAT IS

Byron Katie might have the most repetitive and most interesting job in the world. As a sought-after speaker and bestselling author, she frequently coaches people on their relationships with others. Her premise is that freedom and peace in our relationships with others (and in life) is a matter of deliberate curation of our thoughts and internal narratives. As Katie puts it: "I discovered that when I believed my thoughts, I suffered, but that when I didn't believe them, I didn't suffer, and that this is true for every human being. Freedom is as simple as that."[42]

In her book, *Loving What Is: Four Questions That Can Change Your Life*, Byron Katie outlines her simple but powerful approach.

---

[42] Byron Katie and Stephen Mitchell, *A Thousand Names for Joy: Living in Harmony with the Way Things Are* (New York: Harmony Books, 2007), x.

Her coaching is a guided journey of exploring the narratives and internal beliefs that are holding people back. We all have them! Even though each person is unique and the experiences vary widely, Katie asks the same four questions every time:

1. Is it true?

2. Can you absolutely know it's true?

3. How do you react when you believe that thought?

4. Who would you be without the thought?[43]

You can test this out right now. Think about a relationship or situation where you feel stress. Grab a piece of paper and write down the name of that person or the summary of what is going on, along with the accompanying thoughts that are causing you stress. Then get quiet and still, and ask yourself the four questions. Pause after each one and write down the thoughts you have. Byron Katie's website shares additional tips and even some downloadable resources to help you do this work.[44]

Let's take a trivial and cliché example. You're driving on the freeway, and you notice a car coming up fast behind you. It follows you more closely than you would like, then swerves into the next lane, speeds past you, and cuts right in front of you. Your heart is racing and your brain is filled with adrenaline. If you're like me, you're thinking, "That guy is a jerk."

Now we can walk through the questions. Is it true that the driver of that car is a jerk? I don't know him or anything about his story. I'm already faltering, but then I remember the genuine

---

[43] Byron Katie and Stephen Mitchell, *Loving What Is: Four Questions That Can Change Your Life* (New York: Harmony Books, 2002), 15.

[44] https://thework.com/instruction-the-work-byron-katie/.

terror that flashed through my body when his car came so close, unnecessarily endangering my life and many others, and probably just for his own ego and vanity. Yes, it's true. It's got to be.

Can I absolutely know it's true that the guy is a jerk? Well, no, not really. I might spend a minute constructing possible explanations. Maybe he's racing to the hospital to see a loved one who was injured. Maybe he just lost his job and he's an emotional wreck. If there are any other ways to interpret the behavior (and there always are), then I cannot be absolutely sure my negative label is correct.

For the third question, I get to take a deep look inside myself. How am I reacting when I think about my story that the driver of this car is a jerk? I'm angry—outraged, really—about the injustice of endangering people through careless driving. I am frustrated, threatened, I feel helpless, and I become trapped in a self-perpetuating cycle of negative thoughts and emotions.

Finally, I explore who I would be without the thought. I imagine myself feeling peace, stemming from a profound acceptance and even love of "what is," as opposed to spinning my wheels and raging about how I believe things ought to be. I let go of anger, fear, resentment, frustration, and animosity. I am free to love and to learn, experiencing the full power of Starting with Heart.

## GETTING OUT OF THE BOX

Another helpful framework for thinking about Start with Heart appears in the book *Leadership and Self-Deception* by The Arbinger Institute. The authors introduce the visual of an imaginary box that shapes our every interaction and limits our ability to see clearly. "Being in the box" is to be trapped by false narratives about another person. It's not that we like it—the confines of the box bring conflict, mistrust, and dysfunction to our relationships. But we deceive ourselves into believing the exact things that prevent freedom and peace.

The book frames the idea of the box in terms of business, arguing that organizations will be more successful if the culture is free from harmful narratives. "When you're in the box, people follow you, if at all, only through force or threat of force. But that's not leadership. That's coercion. The leaders that people choose to follow are the leaders who are out of the box."[45]

But being in the box is more than sound business advice, a leadership technique, or a hack to influence people. It's about changing your core. As the Arbinger Institute points out, "people primarily respond not to what we do but to how we're being— whether we're in or out of the box toward them."[46]

This is a shift that goes all the way inward. It's about who we are and how we see other people. To illustrate the point, the book uses examples from everyday life. For example, imagine you are sleeping soundly after a busy day at work when you are awakened by the cries of your newborn baby. You think about getting up and tending to the child, but you decide against it, roll over, and pretend to sleep, hoping your spouse will get up and handle it.

After this initial act of betraying what you know to be right, your brain kicks into gear to justify yourself. You think about how hard you work at your job, and all the times you made sacrifices for the baby in the past week. You think about the big meeting you have coming up, only six hours from now, and how it's your duty to the family to be rested so you can crush that meeting and continue to provide income. Interestingly, this box of self-deception requires a villain, and as the baby keeps crying, your thoughts turn to attack your spouse. You start with

---

[45] The Arbinger Institute, *Leadership and Self-Deception: Getting Out of the Box* (San Francisco: Berrett-Koehler Publishers, 2010), 160.

[46] *Leadership and Self-Deception*, 44.

gentle annoyance that they won't get up, then move to vicious accusations like they are pretending to sleep in order to make you get up, and finally resort to sweeping generalities about how lazy and ungrateful your spouse is.

All of this is happening in your own mind, with no change in the external circumstances. Ironically, you are choosing the exact same bad behaviors of which you are accusing your spouse! You've landed squarely in the box, and your words and actions toward your spouse are likely to reflect it.

Being in the box is seeing others as objects and not as people. It's a frame of mind that feels very real even though it's all invented by our own brains, and it's tricky because the self-deception compounds to make it increasingly hard to see what we are doing. Literally everyone slips into this mental trap. You're probably in the box right now, whether with a partner, child, friend, sibling, parent, coworker, or casual acquaintance. Many people spend decades or even a lifetime in the box, blaming others for their misery and missing countless opportunities for learning.

The good news is that we don't have to stay in the box. There is a way out, and even though it's uncomfortable (see Learning > Comfort), it is worth the effort because of the richness of a life lived in connection with others. You'll recognize this process as a learning loop, similar to the examples we have explored in previous chapters.

## 1. NOTICE

As you think about the simple concept of being in the box, you may start to notice ways in which your inward mindset is viewing people around you as something other than human. Is this employee one of many problems on my list today? Is my child an insurgent seeking to destabilize the family regime? Is this lady with the 100 coupons in the grocery store checkout part of a master conspiracy to make me late for everything and lose my mind? In each of these examples, I am seeing something other than a human.

Watch for signs of "us versus them" thinking. Is there a group or division at work that is automatically the enemy? Do I assume I understand the motives and beliefs of another based on the clothes they wear or the color of their skin?

If you're paying attention, you will start to notice the thoughts and narratives your brain is laying down to demonize the other person and justify you. We all do this. Just seeing it is the first step to getting out.

## 2. ASK

The reflections in Step 1 will often lead to the uncomfortable discovery that you are in the box for a specific relationship. As a result, you are limited in what you can see and understand.

Now is the time to ask questions. Your sole goal is to learn about the experience of another person. It's inherently humanizing to ask a sincere and open question. You wouldn't ask a tree or a goldfish about their experience or perspective. Fighting off the impulse to interrupt, to impose your own narrative, or to "fix" the problems of another, listening not only fosters connection but also forces you to get out of the box. Good questions are key to any kind of learning, and this is especially true about learning with and from other people.

## 3. ACT

With a fresh perspective and new information, you are ready to engage with other people in a way that is free from internal narratives and judgments. Brené Brown refers to this posture as "wholeheartedness." It's a way of living that aligns perfectly with the Start with Heart value.

As you engage with people in the real world, it won't take long for you to be reminded of the natural tendency in yourself and others to slip back into the box. Watching for moments of intuition and instinct and acting on the human decency you feel, you can avoid the self-betrayal that would move you to confinement in the box. It will be a process of learning and trying and slipping back and moving forward that will last a lifetime.

By now, you should have a solid understanding of what I mean by "Start with Heart," along with some frameworks to help you implement it. Hopefully you can see how genuine connection with other people is critical for an empowered learner. Let's wrap up this section with a few actionable tips for Starting with Heart.

## How to Start with Heart

Even though this value can feel very abstract, inward, and even fluffy, Starting with Heart is a very real way to engage with others. True, you will need to change some of your core programming; it's simply not in our nature to live this way. But there are concrete steps you can take that will increase your likelihood of Starting with Heart. Here are a few of my favorites:

### MEET SOMEONE NEW

Every time I encounter a new person, I am presented with a new opportunity for learning. New people force me out of my comfort zone, break down my biases and stereotypes, and push me to see the shared humanity that makes personality and cultural differences feel small and insignificant. Meeting new people could entail conversations with strangers in our day-to-day, active participation in a community, or traveling to unfamiliar places.

As a church missionary, I spent a couple years in Lisbon, Portugal. I have fond memories of walking cobblestone streets, cheering for the national football team, tasting the traditional salted codfish, and ducking into ancient door frames that measured a full foot and half shorter than me. One of my favorite things about my time in Portugal was the friendships I made with the old ladies. Bustling about every day in their black mourning garb, these widows taught me so much about hard work and determined optimism in the face of health challenges and loneliness.

## ASK QUESTIONS FOR WHICH YOU DON'T HAVE ANSWERS

Asking a good question and listening to the answer is one of the best ways to Start with Heart. It forces you into a spirit of curiosity because you cannot simultaneously listen in earnest and cling tightly to your own narrative.

In the early days of Prenda, I introduced the kids to Socratic dialogue as a mode of learning and collaboration. It was fascinating to see them gradually take ownership for this open-ended learning experience with an uncertain outcome. I noticed a strong resistance to open questions, as the kids (like all of us) felt a strong preference for material they already knew and understood. I set a rule that each participant in the discussion had to bring three questions to which they did not have an answer in mind. Often, these questions explored the reactions and thoughts of other participants in the discussion.

## SEEK CONNECTION IN THE MUNDANE

We might want our great moments to shine and sparkle with dramatic meaning, but the truth is that life is lived in the small and seemingly insignificant moments that happen to all of us, every day. It is in these mundane experiences that lasting friendships and meaningful relationships take shape.

I spent the summer of 2002 in Mozambique. Flying twenty-four hours to the other side of the world, I pictured my experience being quixotic, full of the charms of travel. I imagined safaris and pristine beaches and grand adventures. But as I wandered around Maputo, it was the normal, basic things that really mattered. I bought an orange from a roadside stand, got sticky juice all over, and I asked some kids to teach me how to say "Can I have water to wash my hands" in the local Changana dialect. I rode around town in little vans packed with commuters. I played checkers in the city square. Each of these moments was small and insignificant, but as I look back, I realize I was connecting with human beings and learning from them.

## HELP SOMEONE WITHOUT HOPE OF RECIPROCATION

In the hustle and bustle of modern life, it is too easy to slip into a transactional model with other people. You see this in business; an overt quid pro quo that dehumanizes the workplace and discourages genuine connection. Even philanthropic endeavors are too often calculated and tied to some form of self-service.

Instead, you can Start with Heart by deliberately helping someone that has no way of reciprocating. Better if they don't even know! Go pack meals for hungry kids and then refrain from posting about it on social media. Donate anonymously. Pay for the car behind you in the Chick-fil-A drive thru. None of these actions is going to have an impact in the grand scheme of things, but they might help you see the people around you as humans.

Starting with Heart is a powerful way to be an empowered learner. It might also be the hardest of the core values to put into practice. There is always room to grow. Instead of feeling despondent that you haven't yet attained perfection, you can take each interaction as a chance to get better at seeing the humans around you.

# Start with Heart in Action

CHOOSE ONE RELATIONSHIP IN YOUR LIFE WHERE YOU FEEL SOME STRESS or friction. It doesn't have to be dramatic, just a place where you realize you could be closer. Ask yourself how you are seeing the other person:

- Do I see a human being of infinite value?

- Do I see a human being with unlimited potential?

Thinking about the implications of seeing another person in this way, try the four questions framework from Byron Katie or "Getting Out of the Box" from the Arbinger Institute.

Find one thing from the list of ways to Start with Heart that you will try out this week.

# Start with Heart Vignette:

## Kaity's story

I WAS MIDWAY THROUGH MY FIRST MICROSCHOOL SEMESTER WHEN I GOT a cryptic message over Facebook. With a little research, I figured out that the sender of this message developed curricula for a local private school, had an advanced degree in speech pathology and ran a blog about the core principles of successful learning. I immediately wondered what she had in mind. Before long, I found myself sitting at my kitchen table with Kaity Broadbent, geeking out about student-centered learning and listening to her explain the merits of phonics-based reading instruction.

This could have been like most of my Prenda meetings at the time—interesting and engaging, but not really leading anywhere. But there was something different about Kaity. It came across as a ferocity in her eyes and a zealous enthusiasm about the science of humans learning to read. It was obvious that she was interested in the topic, but there was something else going on. It felt almost personal.

As I got to know Kaity, I found out that her passion for helping children learn to read was indeed personal. She was fiercely devoted to her own children and countless others from her community. She was the go-to expert on literacy for a large number of moms and gave out free advice all the time. Within a few weeks, I was asking Kaity about how the Prenda model could be adapted to work for kindergartners and other pre-readers and begging her to help me build out the learning model.

Over the following years, I found Kaity to be one of the hardest working people I've ever met. She wants to learn everything and feels such urgency to improve that the normal human things like sleep feel like a nuisance. But it wasn't until we were looking for a reading curriculum that I found out what was driving Kaity.

Prenda's model is based on a concept called mastery, where each learner operates at their learning frontier and only moves onto the next topic when they have mastered the last one. For the older kids, we facilitate this type of personalized learning and measurement of mastery through adaptive learning tools delivered through the computer. But that doesn't work for a child who hasn't yet learned how to read. What could we do?

Kaity launched a search for early literacy programs that might fit with Prenda. Strong phonics foundation, student-led, mostly offline with plenty of meaningful application opportunities, and mastery tracking without requiring a reading expert to be sitting in the room. As you can imagine, a product that checked all these boxes was hard to come by, and Kaity returned with good news and bad news.

The bad news? Kaity couldn't find a reading curriculum that met all our needs. *That's okay,* I thought. *We can just stick to older students, I guess.* But Kaity had other plans. She had met these kids. Parents who loved Prenda were pleading for a microschool concept for their younger children. It wasn't an anonymous market segment; these were real families and real children, and that made it personal.

And so Kaity embarked on a quest to develop a complete reading curriculum. This was no small feat; I've seen entire education companies set up to handle a similar scope. But Kaity worked feverishly, pushing day and night, pulling in help from others at Prenda and drawing on a bedrock understanding of the basic concepts. Before long, she was ready to launch *Treasure Hunt Reading,* a workbook and accompanying self-serve videos that walks young children from the basic alphabet, to the rules of phonics, to blending sounds, to strong reading comprehension. We used the program to open up microschools to younger learners, and at Kaity's insistence, we also made *Treasure Hunt Reading* available for free to anyone who wants it, whether or not they are signed up with Prenda. Today, thousands of children are using it to learn how to read while simultaneously becoming empowered learners.

I've been in the room when a parent or a child recognizes Kaity from the *Treasure Hunt* videos. It's a remarkable thing. No one sees the countless hours of frantic work, the late-night tears, and the people pushing for deadlines, driving for high quality, and redoing the entire project to incorporate feedback. But somehow, they know that Kaity is a person who Starts with Heart. She cares about each child. She sees them as humans with infinite value and unlimited potential. It's this perspective, running so deep in her core, that helps Kaity accomplish things most of us would find impossible.

# Chapter 6

# Foundation of Trust

THE PRENDA MICROSCHOOL IN MY HOUSE WAS IN FULL SESSION. A group of energetic kids from kindergarten to second grade had trickled in and convened with a yoga meditation in our living room. Each of the children shared their goals and aspirations for the day in a connecting circle, and now it was time to grab the Chromebooks and get started on their learning tutorials.

As the learning guide for this microschool, my wife Kim knew each child well. She could easily see who was feeling off and drill into the underlying emotional and motivational challenges. She knew the various languages the children used to communicate that they were stuck or struggling.

It wasn't surprising, then, for Kim to notice that Noah was being a little more squirrely than usual. She walked over to find him stuck on a reading exercise in the learning software. She knew the backstory: Noah has struggled with learning to read. As a second grader, this is not uncommon, but with a sister who was a superstar reader and a series of teachers who applied less-than-helpful labels, Noah had come to believe the narrative that he simply wasn't cut out for reading. Assuming he would never get it, he had no real incentive to try. Each failed attempt simply reinforced the core narrative and discouraged him from taking any further risks. Noah turned to his natural charisma, fun personality, and adorable smile as means of escape from the painful cycle of trying and failing to read.

At this moment, all of this was on full display. Noah was cracking jokes and getting rewarded with laughter and silliness in a room full of his peers. He was haphazardly clicking on random answers when the software asked him to identify the word he was hearing in his headphones. If he was hurting or upset, he didn't show it. The kid seemed to be having the time of his life, flouting the entire idea of literacy and inviting everyone around him to join him on this path of fun and games.

Kim approached Noah, sat down to be at eye level, and asked in a nonjudgmental way how he was doing. After a silly response, she redirected and invited Noah to engage with the tutorial. She watched him answer questions without thinking, then asked him about it. She reminded him that the way through this particular concept was to learn it; with effort, he could master this lesson and move on to other subjects. She could see the wheels turning as these ideas landed with Noah, but there was still a resistance. Something deeper was holding Noah back.

"Why do you think I want you to learn how to read?" she asked him.

Without even looking at her, Noah resorted to joking: "Because you hate me!"

Noah meant it as a joke. He had spent months in our home, and he knew Kim to be a safe adult who knew him well and most certainly did not hate him. But as the saying goes, there is truth in every joke, and Noah was revealing a bit of his storyline: he was deficient, broken, and a roadblock to the adults in his life, who would love him more if he finally learned how to read.

Kim addressed him directly and made it clear that she did not hate him and so that couldn't be the reason she wanted him to read. "Do you have any other ideas?"

Kim then said, "I want you to learn how to read because I care about you, and learning how to read will help you in your life."

Noah pushed back. He avoided eye contact. He clicked random buttons. When he finally held her gaze, Kim noticed tears welling up in his eyes. She repeated herself. "Noah, I care about you."

I care about you.

Beneath the specific tutorial, beneath the phonograms, beneath the pedagogy, beneath the disruptive behavior and natural charm and silly second-grade jokes, there was a boy that needed to feel loved and safe.

As this need was met, Noah broke down into tears. He accepted that Kim would care about him whether or not he learned how to read. He stopped joking and opened up about his struggles. Eventually, he was ready to get back into the tutorial. This time, he had the security of a caring adult and a space where taking risks and making mistakes are natural and expected parts of the learning process. With this trust in place, Noah was ready to learn how to read. It didn't happen all at once, but he made steady progress through the year and eventually accomplished all his goals.

## What Is Foundation of Trust?

Just like a building needs a solid block of concrete to stand on, learning requires a foundation. And while it's easy and natural to focus on the external behaviors and achievements, the most important foundational element in learning is trust. This is true because learning is an act of faith; you have to believe that the effort you put in, the sacrifices you make, and the inevitable pain and struggle will all be worth it. Learning is uncomfortable and our brains resist it as an unnecessary risk. But on the other side of the hardship is something better.

You can think of Foundation of Trust as a prerequisite for all the learning values we have already discussed. It's hard to Dare Greatly, Figure It Out, Start with Heart and choose Learning > Comfort when you have crippling questions about your core identity and psychological safety.

One interesting attempt to define trust is a mathematical approach by psychologist John Gottman. His research team filmed couples having fifteen-minute conversations. Afterward, he played the video for the couples and gave each partner a dial to rate the interaction. In most cases, Gottman found that the emotional response to the interaction moved together. Both parties felt happy or distressed, depending on how the conversation was going. But in some cases (11 percent), the graphs moved in an inverse pattern. When one partner was feeling down, the other was up, and vice versa. These data reveal a zero-sum mentality in the relationship, where "I win if you lose."

The research team found this particular type of brokenness to run directly opposite from the trust partners need to make a strong relationship. "On the other hand, by trust we really mean, mathematically, that our partner's behavior is acting to increase our rating dial. Even though we're disagreeing, my wife is thinking about my welfare, my best interests." According to this research, trust is a mutual feeling of positive regard and good intentions. It is a confidence that you are both seeking good things for each other. Years later, when the researchers tried to contact the test couples for follow up, they were surprised to find that the men in the low-trust relationships were three times more likely to die early! Trust can have a direct impact on our well-being.[47]

Foundation of Trust is the natural counterpart to Start with Heart. As explained in the last chapter, Start with Heart is about

---

[47] John Gottman, "John Gottman on Trust and Betrayal," *Greater Good Magazine*, October 29, 2011, https://greatergood.berkeley.edu/article/item/john_gottman_on_trust_and_betrayal.

the inward perspective and posture we choose in our perception of others. Foundation of Trust is strongest when we believe that others are Starting with Heart relative to us.

Simple, right?

Of course not! You have lived long enough to know that people are not all safe, that intentions are not all good, and that trust is not only difficult, but dangerous. I agree! Foundation of Trust is not an attempt to deliberately close our eyes to the harsh reality and ugliness that surrounds us. Instead, it's a proactive approach, an explicit focus on trust between people and a constant effort to improve it.

## Why Should I Care?

Maybe you are convinced that perpetually striving for higher levels of trust with the people around you is well worth the effort. But you might be thinking along the lines of Siggy from my favorite movie, *What About Bob*: "With all the horror going on in the world, what difference does it make?"

I could spend the rest of this book exploring the metaphysics behind this question, but instead I will make two simple claims. Trust is critical to learning, and trust is critical to achieving.

### TRUST AND LEARNING

As we just saw in Noah's story, trust is critical for anyone embarking on the learning process. It feels scary not to know something. It takes work to learn it. If I am worried about what people around me think of me, especially those with hierarchical authority, I am unlikely to step onto shaky ground. Instead, we find ways to go through the motions without ever taking the risk of real learning. Every day, millions of people successfully hide from impactful learning, from young children in school to corporate middle managers.

Just as we discussed in the chapter on Learning > Comfort, the reason lies in our brains. In one brain model, scientists talk about three separate structures operating simultaneously in our brains. Sometimes these are referred to as "three brains."

1. Reptilian brain (basal ganglia and brain stem), sometimes referred to as "lizard brain," is the part of our processing that is automatic and directly tied to survival and reproduction. Our reptilian brain makes the lightning decision between "fight or flight."

2. Mammalian brain (amygdala, hippocampus, and cingulate gyrus), or limbic system, is the primary center of our feelings and emotions. This is the part of the brain lighting up when we are angry, discouraged, or exuberant.

3. Primate brain (prefrontal cortex) is where most of our thinking happens. This is the larger and more evolved part of the brain, differentiating us from other animals. Imaging studies can literally see the neurons in the prefrontal cortex firing when human subjects solve problems, think creatively, and exercise our executive functions.[48]

Even though the three brain model has been disproven from an evolutionary biology standpoint, we can all identify with thinking and feeling at all three levels, and the model can be a useful construct for making sense of our own processing. By combining this picture of the three brain systems with the earlier

---

[48] For example: David T. Jones and Jonathan Graff-Radford, "Executive Dysfunction and the Prefrontal Cortex," *Behavioral Neurology and Psychiatry* 27, no. 6 (December 2021): 1586–1601, https://doi.org/10.1212/CON.0000000000001009.

point that our brain is obsessed with saving energy, we can see why trust is so crucial to learning.

Imagine you're given a tricky arithmetic problem. You might imagine yourself seated at a table with a pencil and scratch paper. You've eaten a wholesome breakfast and your life is abundant with people who care about you. Depending on the problem and your previous exposure to arithmetic, this situation could be pleasant or challenging.

But now imagine you have the same problem, but you are running for your life from a hungry predator. Your reptilian brain kicks in, overriding other brain systems, stealing the blood flow and energy to prioritize basic survival. It's next to impossible to solve the math problem.

Interestingly, a similar fight for resources occurs when our limbic system sets in, demanding energy to process the emotions we feel. Try solving the math problem if you are mad at a family member, and you'll find a similar difficulty. Our highest human abilities to think and reason are rendered almost useless when we are in fight or flight mode or experiencing extreme emotions.

If we want to grow our brains as empowered learners, we need some way to quiet these natural forces. Trust with the people around us accomplishes this, placating our reptilian and mammalian brains so that we can think, create, reason, and learn. At the physical level, I need to believe that my life is not on the line. But trust runs deeper than that. In order to unlock the full learning potential of my advanced prefrontal cortex, I need to believe that I am safe emotionally as well.

If I want to be an empowered learner, I need to deliberately seek out and create trust.

## TRUST AND ACHIEVEMENT

So far, we've talked extensively about learning in a personal capacity. But often the mountains we choose to climb will be collective, like making your marriage better or building a micro-school. In those cases, you cannot separate trust and achievement because those goals involve other people—trust enables success.

Trust has been extensively studied in the area of business. In their 2006 book, Stephen M. R. Covey and Rebecca Merrill argue that the organizations cannot move faster than the "Speed of Trust," just like objects in the physical world cannot exceed the speed of light. According to the subtitle, trust is "the one thing that changes everything."

Airbnb Founder and CEO Brian Chesky unpacks how this works: "The stronger the culture, the less corporate process a company needs. When the culture is strong, you can trust everyone to do the right thing. People can be independent and autonomous. They can be entrepreneurial."[49] Strong culture is a shared sense of understanding what we are all about and how we agree to behave. It is about trust.

Netflix is known for having one of the strongest company cultures around. They released a 129-slide "culture deck" in 2009 that describes not only *what* the company believes and expects, but *why*.[50] Many of the ideas are drastically different from what you would find in other companies. The deliberate culture implemented at Netflix has helped the company succeed through multiple technology iterations and economic cycles.

This culture is based on hiring great people and extending them a lot of trust. One new vice president at the company was surprised at the level of transparency and the willingness of

---

[49] Brian Chesky, "Don't Fuck Up the Culture," Medium, April 24, 2020, https://medium.com/@bchesky/dont-fuck-up-the-culture-597cde9ee9d4.

[50] An archived version of this can be found online: Reed Hastings, "Culture (Original 2009 Version)," SlideShare, June 30, 2011, https://www.slideshare.net/reed2001/culture-2009.

senior leaders to own mistakes. All of this fosters trust. He said, "Netflix treats employees like adults who can handle difficult information and I love that. This creates enormous feelings of commitment and buy-in from employees."[51]

The verdict is clear: deliberate emphasis on building high levels of trust is key to business success. But it extends beyond that, to any endeavor that involves other people. Marriage, family, community, civics. In each of these areas, our ability to achieve will be directly related to the level of trust we feel for others and they feel for us.

## How to Build a Foundation of Trust

Trust is critical to our success as learners, and in achieving the goals we set with others. But how do you go about building trust? There is a whole world of research on this. Instead of trying to summarize it all, I will choose my favorite insights and invite you to continue your quest to build more trust.

### TAKE OWNERSHIP

It's the most natural thing in the world to make excuses, blame others, and slip into a victim mentality. We all know from experience how messy and complicated human interactions can be. Perhaps you feel betrayed by a past interaction. Maybe you have a narrative about a person that makes it simply inconceivable to consider trusting them. The culture around you could be so low in trust that you will simply be pushed around if you start trying to trust people. After all, you gotta look out for number one!

But even with the messiness of life, there is tremendous trust-building power in taking ownership. Jocko Willink and

---

[51] Reed Hastings and Erin Meyer, *No Rules Rules: Netflix and the Culture of Reinvention* (New York: Penguin Press, 2020).

Leif Babin take this concept to the extreme with their book, *Extreme Ownership*, pulling from their experience with high-trust teams in combat.

## SET BOUNDARIES

Even as you move toward a stronger sense of ownership, it is unwise to blindly trust every scammer that calls your cell phone.

Trust goes hand in hand with boundaries. Each relationship in our lives exists within a set of boundaries, whether stated or implied. Thinking about boundaries and communicating them clearly is an important step to building trust, helping us avoid the painful trust-breaking or broken assumptions. For example, if someone in your immediate family is addicted to drugs, it is probably a bad idea to give them large amounts of money. Instead, you might communicate your love and delineate the things you are willing to provide to help them. Starting with Heart and building a Foundation of Trust are best lived within clear rules and boundaries.

Setting boundaries creates the freedom to take full ownership of your part of the equation. I can always decide to see the infinite value and unlimited potential in another person. I can always choose to address trust issues in an open and honest conversation. I can always extend respect and generosity toward someone else, whether I am in their presence or not. By identifying the parts I can control and setting clear boundaries for the parts I can't, I can take ownership.

## PUT TRUST ON THE TABLE

One approach to improving Foundation of Trust is to make it an explicit focus. When we talk about Foundation of Trust as coworkers at Prenda, we think of it as something tangible, like you could hold it in your hands, examine it, or set it on the table. If we are both Starting with Heart, then we can have a constructive conversation about increasing the level of trust between us. We can share openly about the words and behaviors that make trust more difficult, and we can help each other see the specific actions we could take to improve trust.

Kassidi was one of the early employees at Prenda. She came highly recommended, and she quickly proved herself by taming the chaos of the financial and operational parts of the fast-growing business. We didn't know each other very well, so it was a little tense when we ran into some sensitive questions around compensation and equity. I had made a decision, and in Kassidi's opinion, that decision was unconventional and self-serving.

Without a strong Foundation of Trust between us, and wanting to sanity-check her instincts, Kassidi took the issue to a personal attorney she had worked with in the past. When she came back to me with the opinion of this outside attorney, I felt offended that she handled the issue this way instead of bringing it to me.

As you could imagine, trust was strained on both sides of this relationship. Kassidi and I could have accepted that and moved forward with a weak Foundation of Trust. But instead, we decided to address it directly. Kassidi shared how my initial decision had weakened her trust in me. I explained how her approach to the situation weakened my trust in her. We both cried. This stuff is hard. In the end, we agreed that we both wanted to operate at a higher level of trust, and that a strong Foundation of Trust would be best for the company. I ended up collecting some more input and reversing the decision.

Since that day several years ago, Kassidi and I have continued to build trust. We do the relationship hygiene things that keep trust high, like taking an interest in each other's personal lives, extending support during challenging times, and addressing issues as they come up instead of letting them fester. She recently called me out on being distracted with my phone during Zoom calls—and she was right! I trust Kassidi to run the finances of the company, including running multimillion-dollar deals. She trusts me to treat her and everyone fairly.

## REMOVE THE ARMOR

Author and researcher Brené Brown has built a career teaching people to be vulnerable. In a 2010 TED Talk that has been viewed 58 million times, Brené explains how "excruciating vulnerability" is the only antidote to the shame and fear we all experience.[52] She studied thousands of people who are able to form the genuine connections that add meaning and purpose to life, and found that "these are whole-hearted people living from a deep sense of worthiness."

Brené talks about the behaviors, habits, and mindsets that get in the way of authentic connection and whole-hearted living, comparing them to psychological armor we put on to protect our feelings.[53] Maybe we show up as a "knower" instead of a learner, concealing our fear and shame that other people might not find us valuable enough. Anything we do to pretend, posture, and protect puts a barrier between us and others, killing our chances of real trust and connection.

This concept applies to our efforts to learn with others. If I enter an encounter with no trust in you, I will remain distant. Kids use strategies like shutting down or acting out, but all of us have some version of these protective mechanisms. From that

---

[52] Brené Brown, "The Power of Vulnerability," TEDxHouston, December 23, 2010, video, 20:03, https://www.ted.com/talks/brene_brown_the_power_of_vulnerability?language=en.

[53] Brené Brown, "Armored versus Daring Leadership, part 1 of 2," April 5, 2021, in *Dare to Lead with Brené Brown*, podcast, 39:31, https://brenebrown.com/podcast/brene-on-armored -versus-daring-leadership-part-1-of-2/.

place behind the armor, I cannot learn anything because I won't even admit that there is something I want to know.

Instead, empowered learners are deliberate about setting aside the armor and opening themselves up; not only to fear and pain, but to connection and learning and joy. It's a scary thing to do, but it is the only way to build a Foundation of Trust.

At one of our leadership meetings, we did an activity where each member of the team provided feedback for each other person using the "Start, Stop, Continue" framework. I had prepared some feedback for Kaity, our Head of Learning and longtime leader at Prenda, that I knew would not surprise her because it lined up with past conversations, but I also knew it was a sensitive spot and I wondered how it would land.

As we sat together to review the feedback, both of us were leaning in. Clarifying questions, additional context, and rising emotions took us to a familiar place where it felt frustrating to both of us. But instead of getting stuck in a rut, piling on more psychological armor, or making a joke to diffuse the tension, Kaity helped me understand something important. She showed me how my habit of questioning her work, challenging her assumptions, and suggesting alternate approaches was communicating something very different, something I never intended. She said, "What I hear is that I am not good enough."

It was a vulnerable moment. Kaity had removed any armor and shared in a way that was direct and brave, and I was able to see that deep fear and feel it with her. It led to a great conversation about how we both feel like imposters, how I see her true value and potential, noticing all the growth over years of working together, and how I can do a better job separating thoughts about the work from opinions about the person. We walked away with a stronger trust, and it all started with a vulnerable moment where Kaity removed the armor and shared her deepest self.

## TELL THE TRUTH

Honest and open communication is critical for a high-trust relationship. If you sense that another person is telling you what you want to hear, but you suspect they are saying very different things to other people, you are likely to feel a reduction in trust. Our internal meters for authenticity are remarkable; not only can we detect cases of blatant falseness, but we intuitively understand if someone is massaging the truth.

In a recent article in the *Harvard Business Review*, Ed Batista makes the case for a "feedback-rich culture."[54] Important in the workplace, the home, the classroom, and any other learning environment, trust is higher when we speak candidly. When something is wrong, we address it directly with a courageous optimism that we can figure it out. When someone violates a norm or lets down the team, we talk to them about it. All of this is modeled by leaders and reinforced with a steady flow of positive feedback, constantly recognizing and validating the many things that are going well.

I learned this lesson in a conversation with Cahlan, a close friend and one of the original people helping with Prenda. It had been a rough couple of months, and Cahlan was feeling the load. A four-fold increase in the number of students and very fast hiring had shifted his role from entrepreneurial problem-solving to leading leaders and running a large organization. At the same time, I was pushing for greater clarity on the vision and strategy of the company and asking Cahlan to help. The pressure kept building until it reached a breaking point, and we found ourselves face to face for a challenging conversation, the type Brené Brown calls a "rumble."

After checking in as people, reviewing the business issues, and talking about organizational challenges, it was clear that

---

[54] Ed Batista, "Building a Feedback-Rich Culture," *Harvard Business Review*, December 24, 2013, https://hbr.org/2013/12/building-a-feedback-rich-culture.

Cahlan had more to say. He opened up about the experience he was having. It is hard to hear directly from a person you care about that you are causing them pain, but it had to be said. Cahlan told me, "You can be really demanding, and your high expectations can make you difficult to work with." It was direct, honest, and exactly what I needed to hear. During this time of stressful growing pains, I had prioritized the mission and the work over the sanity and well-being of people, and that led directly to burnout. As a result of Cahlan's willingness to tell the truth, I was able to trust him to point out my blind spots and help me improve. His trust in me increased as well because he saw that I genuinely cared about him and wanted the truth.

Hearing the truth in this way can definitely hurt. But it also leads to higher trust and shines lights on the problems that need fixing. Telling the truth is the only way to ensure high trust, even if it's painful. That's because the truth shines light on false assumptions, posturing, gossiping, and many other forms of trust-eroding communication.

## A Word of Caution

Trust is critical for all the good things we want in our interactions and learning with other humans. But it can also be counterfeit and exploited for evil. Foundation of Trust can be done in a shady, manipulative way. To make sure you earn the trust of others, there is a simple question you can ask: what is my goal in addressing trust between us?

Now look at your answer. If you are certain in your diagnosis that the problem is the other person's fault, and you know exactly how they could change in a way that would fix the problem, then you are not in the right frame of mind to address trust. Building trust authentically requires openness and curiosity, assuming good intentions in others.

Instead, try to think of alternate explanations for what is going on. Keep listing them until you convince yourself that you don't know what the other person is experiencing in the relationship. Now you're ready to ask honest questions and you're curious enough to listen to the answers. Never use Foundation of Trust to "get what you want" from another person.

# Foundation of Trust in Action

LIVING THE FOUNDATION OF TRUST VALUE IS AN ONGOING QUEST. You're never really done, because there are always ways to increase trust in the relationships in your life. But striving for greater trust with the people around you is worth it because it unlocks meaning and fulfillment and opens you up to all kinds of learning.

To improve your Foundation of Trust, choose a relationship where you want higher trust. Ask these questions:

1. How do I see this person? In other words, am I Starting with Heart?

2. How do I think this person sees me? Get clear in your head about your internal narratives and question them.

3. Usually, Foundation of Trust conversations follow a conflict or miscommunication. Get clear on what you are assuming about the intentions of the other person. Then replace those assumptions with honest questions and ask them directly.

4. Check for consistency in your communication. Do you say the same things to a person that you say about them to others?

# Foundation of Trust Vignette:

## Rachelle's Story

THE FIRST TIME I MET RACHELLE, SHE WAS LEAPING ACROSS A BONFIRE. A group of adult chaperones were standing around chatting at a campout for teenagers, and from my vantage point seated near the outer ring, I noticed her staring at the flame with a determined curiosity. The hesitation did not last long. She backed up, smoothed out her old-timey skirt, and ran at the fire, leaping with all her might and just barely skimming the flames at the other side of a six-foot fire ring. A couple years later, I learned that this daredevil curiosity and headfirst approach to challenges was core to Rachelle's being.

At first, I saw it in her efforts to spread the word about Prenda. Rachelle had seen the microschool in my house and quickly caught the vision, laughing out loud when I showed her my original spreadsheet because I was vastly underestimating how Prenda would grow (she was right). Rachelle crisscrossed the State of Arizona, meeting with parents about the microschool concept. She answered their questions, introduced them to each other, and exuded confidence that they were capable of starting a microschool.

Over time, I came to see that the bold leap Rachelle was taking was less about launching new microschools and driving business outcomes and all about trust. I met one person after another who leaned on Rachelle to get through the fears and worries and take a leap to empower learners. Rachelle asked people for trust, not in a perfect organization or a flawless product (just ask anyone who experienced Prenda in those early days), but in a group of people committed to being empowered learners.

Rachelle asked people to trust themselves to start a microschool. She also asked them to trust us, that we would be there helping them. The role of learning guide was brand new—not a teacher in the traditional sense because the guide does not deliver information, design lessons, or evaluate student work, but critical to a successful microschool because one caring adult can be there for children through the messy learning process and set the conditions for empowered learners to grow. Rachelle approached each interaction with such honesty and confidence in the person she was meeting that many people opened up to her about fears, doubts, and worries.

By the time we held our first conference for learning guides in 2019, I was floored to see how many of the guides physically surrounded Rachelle. It was a sign of the psychological safety they felt with her and the high trust that comes with tackling obstacles, learning, and growing.

Things didn't go perfectly, and part of building trust meant owning mistakes and working hard to make things right. I remember a moment where we found out that one of our policies would no longer be admissible under a contract with a partner school. That meant we had to break our promise to some of our learning guides. As Rachelle and I talked it over, we could see only one path forward that honored the trust placed in us. We called forty-one learning guides, one at a time, and explained to them that we needed to break our promise, that we were sorry, and that we were ready to help them in any way we could, even if that meant they no longer wanted to do Prenda.

It was a sobering time. By and large, the guides understood the change and appreciated our candor in communicating with them.

We came out of that challenge—like so many others along the way—with a stronger Foundation of Trust, one that would support collaborating and achieving and learning together for a long time to come.

# Chapter 7

# Making It Real

CONGRATULATIONS! YOU'VE MADE IT THROUGH SIX CHAPTERS AND seen the entire framework. You know what an empowered learner is, and you have the five core values that will help you be one, not just in your individual efforts, but in your interactions with others as well. You've seen examples from great empowered learners from history and from the Prenda story.

I genuinely hope that reading this book has caused you to reflect with curiosity about the role active learning plays in your life. The empowered learner frame has helped me prioritize hard decisions, collaborate with others in deeper and more productive ways, and find the motivation to stick with goals when things are hard.

Hopefully, you have noticed that empowered learners are not some abstract theoretical construct. They are real people, like you and me, who wake up every morning to the same types of obstacles and challenges. By choosing to be an empowered learner, you are adopting a way of life where you see everything and everyone around you as exactly what you need in your learning journey.

## Warnings

As you embark on the path to empowered learning, there are a few things you need to know. My goal in this section is to help you make an informed decision, fully aware of the challenges and pitfalls; I want you to be clear on what empowered learning is *not*. It's kind of like the opposite of a sales pitch. There are no rose-colored glasses here.

### NOT A LIFEHACK

We live in a day of 140 characters and three-minute videos. We like our content neat and tidy, with low investment and a satisfying reward. We swap "lifehacks" about how to save time, win at parenting, and look cool on social media.

Becoming an empowered learner is the opposite of a lifehack. Instead of cute and simple, it is a messy pursuit that lasts a lifetime, filled with ups and downs, heartache and exhilaration. I can guarantee there will be times where you are tired, discouraged, and questioning whether you are meant to be an empowered learner. Expecting those times can make it easier to face them in the moment and give the unequivocal answer: yes, of course I can be an empowered learner! Because you absolutely can.

### AGENCY IS TERRIFYING

You've probably noticed that the entire empowered learner concept centers on a human making a choice. Agency is at the core of the entire approach. Because of that, you should know right up front that *agency is terrifying*. Humans making choices means that there is a real possibility—a certainty, even—that they will make choices we don't agree with. We've already talked about many ways where we undermine our own effort through fear, distractions, and other unhelpful choices.

As we seek to help other people become empowered learners, agency can become almost unbearable. When we allow another person to make a choice, we relinquish control over the outcome, which is really difficult because we care so much.

Pixar's masterpiece *Finding Nemo* captures this point perfectly. After tragically losing his spouse and almost all his offspring, a clownfish named Marlin promises his son, "I'll never let anything happen to you." But as little Nemo grows up, Marlin's pure fatherly desire to protect him becomes the barrier to Nemo's growth, progress, and ultimate happiness. His friend Dory points this out in riveting simplicity: "That's a funny thing to promise. You can't never let *anything* happen to him. Then nothing would *ever* happen to him."

Honoring the agency of another person—especially a person we love—may be the greatest act of counterintuitive faith. It means they will certainly get hurt. Their path may be long and winding. This is equally true when we extend trust to ourselves, owning our decisions and accepting the consequences. Agency is terrifying, but there is no other way for us to learn and grow and to become the people we are capable of being.

## LEARNING IS FOREVER

Here's the thing about seeking learning frontiers: there will always be more to learn. There is always a deeper and more profound understanding available. There is additional knowledge to be gained. There are vital questions in your future that, right now, you don't even know to ask.

This might seem trivial to you now, sitting in comfort and reading a book. But imagine yourself at the end of a hike, reaching the top of a mountain, and then discovering there is another, bigger mountain waiting for you on the other side. This can be exhausting and de-energizing for even the most ardent empowered learner.

Maybe you decide on a mid-career change, putting yourself through additional school at great effort and personal sacrifice. You dream of graduation day, when all your coursework will be behind you and the skies are clear forevermore. But then you start the job search, and you realize the difficulty of finding the right match between your skills and passion and the needs of a business. *This is harder than school,* you might think. Eventually, you land the job and realize that none of the day-to-day activities at work are the same as your degree program. New software tools, new approaches. *I have to learn everything from scratch!* Maybe you take a new role, or the company implements a change, and you are back to square one, just when you were getting the hang of the old way.

Despite what our comfort-seeking brains want to tell us, learning does not have an end date. There is no peaceful ride into the sunset. If we're open to it, we have opportunities to learn every day, every week, every month, every year. And we wouldn't want it any other way.

## Advice

Okay, that felt a little dark. I'm not trying to talk you out of learning. It's the best path you can choose, even though it is not the easy or comfortable one. As we've discussed, this discomfort and opposition is critical to our growth. Resistance makes you stronger in the gym, and this is just as true for developing your brain and yourself.

Now that we've introduced the empowered learner, covered all the principles, and even issued a few warnings, we can finish up with pointed, actionable advice. What is the one thing you could focus on, right now, that would help you be an empowered learner? There is no "one size fits all" answer to that question; you are unique and I would need to know you, talk to you face to face, and hope that together we can identify the next step in your learning journey. But as I thought about key moments in my life where swapping out one core belief for another unlocked (or could have unlocked) exponential learning, I found simple themes that feel applicable to many of us. I've packaged the advice as simple statements you could repeat to remind yourself to be an empowered learner.

## DON'T BE AFRAID

We've already talked about fear, the constant, crippling force opposing every attempt to become an empowered learner. It's real and abiding for everyone, pulling us away from active learning. At times in your learning journey, you might be afraid of the negative emotions you might encounter if you fail. You might fear the opinions of others, especially if they represent the "powers that be" in your culture and institutions. You might find yourself fearing success, feeling like the implications of Daring Greatly take you out of your comfortable but limited self-conception.

Fear is ever-present and sneaky. It is hard to diagnose because the emotional response overrides higher order processing in your brain, and then launches into a stream of flawed reasoning to confirm your fear-based convictions. The first and best way to deal with fear is to call it out directly.

I didn't do this when I ran into fear as a brand new kindergartner. I was so excited to be at school after hearing my mom tell me all about it. Rocking my tall tube socks with colored stripes at the top (it was the 1980s), I showed up with my backpack and a smile and listened as my new teacher introduced us to the world of formal education.

Not long into the semester, I had an experience that made a huge difference in my life. I remember the lights were dimmed because there was a movie playing, and I was sitting at a tiny desk along with other kids. I was using crayons to color a page.

I noticed the teacher walk up to my desk, stand above me, and watch me color. I distinctly remember how huge she seemed and how small I felt. Her face was serious as she told me, "You're doing it wrong." Apparently there was a proper technique to coloring, and I didn't know the right way.

Looking back, the whole thing is so silly and trivial. Who cares about coloring technique? This teacher, who was a very kind person, probably made hundreds of comments to kids that day, and she was nice to me the entire school year. Why did this instance stick with me?

The reason is fear. As a small kid being reprimanded for coloring wrong, I felt complex emotions like frustration and shame. These emotions settled in over the ensuing weeks to become a permanent fear; specifically, I was afraid of getting in trouble. Over thirteen years, all the way to high school graduation, fear was always present. I carefully kept my head down, avoided risks, and never challenged anything. I allowed the structures around me to control me. I thought I was doing the right thing, playing by the rules, going with the flow, and being agreeable. In retrospect, I was allowing my fear to get in the way of my learning.

I'm not saying I wish I had caused a ruckus for its own sake. I happen to be an advocate of civility and collaboration. But as I look back, I wish I could have seen that fear for what it was. I wish I had noticed it, so that when I chose to pursue a big goal or ran into opposition along the way, I could move forward without fear talking me out of it.

On a wall at the Facebook corporate headquarters, in huge block letters, read the words, "What would you do if you weren't afraid?" This question is an excellent tool for identifying the places fear is showing up in your life and limiting your learning. I wish I would have asked myself that question as a kindergartner.

## TURN DOWN THE CHATTER

Have you ever found yourself trying to think or communicate and getting vaguely frustrated because you can't seem to focus? The reason is never clear at first, but after a while you notice that the background noise from the car radio or television ads is loud and annoying. It was there all along, an unrelenting challenge to your productive thinking, but it somehow stayed hidden from your consciousness.

Your brain does the same thing, all the time, but without a physical button you can push to turn it off. In his book *Soundtracks: The Surprising Solution to Overthinking*, Jon Acuff compares the relentless thoughts and chatter in your head to a radio station. Even though you can't turn it off, he says, you have a figurative knob that controls the volume, and you can be deliberate about turning down the chatter.

I had an experience with internal chatter during my sophomore year of high school, when my brain was tuned to a station that wasn't helping. *What are my friends doing this weekend? Why wasn't I invited? Do they think I'm annoying? I said that thing the other day trying to be funny and no one laughed.* The thoughts and stories were filling up my headspace, and I didn't even notice them. I just knew I wasn't happy.

All of this came to a screeching halt one day early in the first semester of tenth grade. I had walked with a group of pre-driving-age friends to the shopping center down the street, where we cobbled together sub sandwiches by purchasing bread for twenty-five cents at Blimpie and meat and cheese for a dollar from the grocery store next door (free mayonnaise and mustard packets!). We walked back together, but my friends were in more of a hurry and I found myself alone, rounding the corner into the school parking lot. I got lost in my thoughts, contemplating my frustrations about high school society and my overall lack of satisfaction.

I remember the exact spot, along the sidewalk next to the football field, where I had a big idea. It arrived so suddenly that I actually stopped walking. *Why do I have to wait for the weekend to be happy? Why does it matter what other people think, or what happens to me? What if I could just be happy, anytime, any place?*

This might sound obvious to you now, but to my tenth grade self it felt like shifting tectonic plates. I realized that I could just decide not to worry about things I couldn't control. I could turn down the volume on the chatter. I could take ownership of my happiness.

From that moment on, high school was a different ballgame. I could just relax, be myself, and set my own terms. I threw out all my preconceived definitions of "cool" and rejected the authority of the implicit hierarchy. I embraced the inner geek that I had previously tried to suppress, competing in math competitions and wearing my Academic Decathlon shirt with pride. I started talking to people, expecting nothing in return except a chance to learn about another human. Paradoxically, my social status rose. Before this moment, I stuck to my small group of "safe" people. After the epiphany, I felt like I could connect with anyone, and that led me to all sorts of beautiful friendships.

## CHOOSE THE GAME

My next piece of advice is to be conscious and proactive about the game you choose to play. Depending on where you are in life, the rules and the players will vary, but there will always be a predominant game. Sometimes the game is simple, like when a sales person tries to exceed targets and outperform the rest of the team. In other cases, the game is harder to discern. For example, new parents might find themselves competing with peers on whose baby sleeps the best, or the relative timing of mobility milestones like crawling and walking.

During high school, I fell in with a set of pretty focused and ambitious students. I learned a lot from my peers—they worked hard, maintained a high standard of integrity, and perfected the art of good, clean fun. We attended a run-of-the-mill public high school, complete with all the standard measures. We compared test scores and grade point averages. It turned into a friendly competition, with all the folklore that comes with it. I remember hearing that my friend Aaron got a near perfect score on the math portion of the SAT, despite falling asleep in the testing center! Each of these friends was well aware of the GPA (grade point average) rankings in our class. Not only were we striving for As in all the courses, we also chose to sign up for advanced courses in order to boost our GPAs. The competition was intense, with hundredths of a point separating first place from second place.

Meanwhile, I was spending a lot of time at the sand volleyball courts. I had discovered a love for volleyball, and I was delighted that my awkward, lanky body actually worked pretty well for spiking and blocking and diving for balls. My junior year was the first time our school district offered a men's volleyball league, and several of my friends tried out for the team.

Given my love for the sport, you'd think I would have done everything I could to get on the volleyball team. But that's not what I did. I didn't even try out! Why not? The short answer is that I had bought into the game of winning the best grade point average. Signing up for a non-advanced class like volleyball would have pulled down my GPA and knocked me down a couple spots in the rankings. Instead, I took an extra engineering class that carried the weight of an advanced course, worked hard to get an A grade, and ended up with a higher academic ranking.

For years, I thought of this as a success story. I might have even been proud of my willingness to give up playing volleyball in sacrifice to the higher good of earning a high GPA.

Now I see it quite differently. I succeeded at playing a game, yes, but was that the game I really wanted to play? I didn't really think about it at the time. Instead, I accepted the structure presented to me and the inherent goals and rules. I played the game without asking whether it was the game I wanted to play. As a result, I missed a chance to get better at volleyball, build strong relationships with teammates, and enjoy the excitement of learning a different form of competition.

The point of this story is not that academics are bad, or that sports are good. The point is that you can choose the game you want to play. You're different than people around you, so there is no reason to assume that their game is the right one for you. It is even less likely that an institution designed hundreds of years ago or administered by people in an office somewhere is perfectly tailored for your learning and growth.

Be careful here. There is nothing wrong with joining an institution or looking for inspiration in other people. College, for example, can play a crucial role in the life and career trajectory of many people. The point is that *you* get to decide. It's *your* choice. Don't blindly allow others to define your course. Recognizing this choice and being deliberate about it is a critical step in becoming an empowered learner.

## TWO SHELVES

As the mindsets and habits of active learning sink in, you may find yourself with many interests, questions, pursuits, goals, and dreams. It's been the challenge of empowered learners for ages. Think about the notebook sketches of Leonardo da Vinci, or the science experiments of Benjamin Franklin—you're in great company!

You know you can't do everything. Realistically, you don't have the time or energy to carry out even a tiny fraction of the possibilities suddenly presenting themselves. But have no fear; there is a simple framework you can use for deciding how to allocate your time.

We've already talked about choosing a mountain in Chapter 2. It seems daunting to choose the right mountain, because it feels like a big decision and you won't ever feel like you have enough information. But the right thing to do is choose one and start climbing, even if you are unsure it's best.

The reason this is the correct approach is that you can change mountains. You can always change your vision or goal to one that fits you better, so you don't need to worry about your current mountain being the wrong one. But how do you consider changes? If you never change your goals, you end up chained to a desk, doing a job you hate. If you change too much, you spend your life in fits and starts, never making the deep and lasting impact that comes with sticking with a goal over time.

This is where the "two shelves" model comes in handy. I was forced to create this simple rule when I graduated from college and found myself torn by the seemingly infinite possibilities of the "real world." I wanted to teach high school physics. I wanted to try documentary filmmaking, and go deep on biofuel production from algae, and maybe work in the front office of a college football program. I had a never-ending flow of entrepreneurial ideas, from a marketplace for short-term contract work in information services (I later discovered ELance.com) to a video game simulating operating a commercial building.

I knew I couldn't dive in and work on all of these things, and I had a stable job and a growing family for which I was the primary breadwinner. But like Shakira, "I want to try everything."

The solution to this problem came as a simple model where I imagine a bookcase with two shelves, stacked on top of a large cabinet. The top shelf represents my main thing. It is what I spend most of my time on, and it's my primary source of livelihood. Hopefully, this is something I enjoy that allows me to create the life I want and provides me with a steady stream of learning opportunities. But it's unlikely that I will get all that, at least not right off the bat.

That's why there is a second shelf. The second shelf creates a space for me to experiment with another mountain while keeping the stability of the first shelf. But the second shelf also helps me focus. There is only space for one thing on the second shelf. Every other idea must wait patiently in the cabinet below, getting no time or effort from me.

With the mental bookshelf assembled, we're ready to put it to use. I'll use an actual example from my life to illustrate.

A few years after leaving graduate school, I had gotten the hang of professional life. I took on assignments, cared about the quality of my work, met deadlines, etc. But I had also come to understand the limits at work, weaved into the decision-making structure, that essentially ruled out a subset of the innovative and/or crazy ideas I was grappling with. The president of the small consulting firm was always willing to chat with me, and in retrospect I marvel at the patience and graciousness he showed to a young upstart with wacky ideas. But even with the chance to learn from this great mentor, I found the pace of my learning to be declining. Without realizing what was happening, my brain started to wander to other domains, and soon I found myself tinkering with an idea for a recipe app (Pandora for dinners, with autogenerated grocery lists). In my time after hours, I called friends and interviewed them about their process of choosing meals. I designed some basic screens and hacked together a working prototype.

During this time moonlighting on the recipe app, I learned two things. First, I was missing a lot of skills that would be necessary to succeed with this new app. For example, I didn't know any frameworks for professional software development.

My prototype was in Microsoft Excel with some Visual Basic macros, way too clunky for a person to actually use. The other thing I learned, as I struggled through software tutorials and encountered an ambiguous response from my target customers, was that I didn't really feel committed to the recipe app idea. It was fun and interesting, and I think it would have solved a problem for people who prefer home-cooked dinners, but it didn't connect at a deep level with who I am and the impact I want to make in the world. Meanwhile, I was embarking on a new area of expertise in my day job and realizing there were other professional opportunities that would unlock the learning I was seeking. Eventually, I stopped working on the app and found a job in the same field with a different type of organization.

In this story, you can see the shelves at work. The top shelf was my full time job, where I worked hard to ensure I was providing all the value expected of me and more. The second shelf was the recipe app. It was a great outlet for my extra energy and forced me to learn things I would not have otherwise encountered. Eventually, I swapped out the recipe app for a new "side project," finding a new job in a different part of the industry. That led to my next top shelf, a new full-time job.

Most of the time, I keep a project on the second shelf for a while before replacing it with another one. These projects vary—writing a children's book (*My First Book of Electromagnetism*), launching a campaign to recruit new restaurants to my city's downtown, supporting my dad's Congressional campaign, trying to bring back a new toy. Occasionally, the side project becomes the main thing, moving from the second shelf to the top shelf. This happened after a few years of running Code Club, when I quit my day job to bring afterschool coding programs to libraries all over.

## LOOK BACKWARD

Another trick for living like a learner is to look backward every once in a while. In your learning journey, you're bound to encounter tough moments and feel discouraged. In those moments, it's a great idea to reflect on your progress. You will notice your growth, and by noticing how far you have come, you will find the motivation to keep going.

There is an apocryphal story that perfectly captures this idea. A young boy was working with his mother on a farm. They were removing weeds by hand, each of them responsible for a row of crops. They started early in the morning, and as the hours went by, the sun heating up and the exhaustion settling in, the boy started to feel despondent. It didn't seem to matter how hard he worked and how long he stuck with it—the row ahead of him seemed infinitely long. He complained to his mother that his muscles were aching and he was making no progress. With a wise smile, the mother advised her son to turn around and look backward. He saw a seemingly infinite row of crops, all neatly weeded over hours of his hard work. Looking backward helped the boy see the progress he made and gave him the confidence to keep going forward.

I learned this lesson in one of the darkest times of my life, when I failed the qualifying exams at MIT. I had entered a couple years previously, embarking on the PhD route that would have led to a career as a professor or a researcher in the field of nuclear fusion. The coursework was grueling, and I battled constant thoughts of overwhelm and inadequacy. All of the students were doing research, and here again, I felt like a loser. I frequently bungled experiments, struggled to troubleshoot the apparatus, and missed insights in the data. Worse, everyone around me seemed to understand what was going on. The other students were adept at tensor notation and statistical methods. The research staff knew exactly how to make the equipment work and read the results.

During all this bumpy time, I found myself hanging on with a determination to grit my teeth and work hard. I trusted that I would eventually succeed if I put in the effort and refused to quit. After all, that recipe had proven successful again and again in other areas of life.

Then came time for the qualifying exams. This time-honored tradition in PhD programs is designed as a sort of filter to protect the very integrity of academia, ensuring that no one enters the realm of scholarship without a deep understanding of the subject matter. I knew it was an uphill climb, but I was determined to be in the top group of students who pass the exams. I studied like a maniac and practiced with friends and classmates. I talked about my research to anyone who would listen. With a hopeful heart, I entered the room for the four-hour written portion, where I was expected to derive key equations governing the motion of charged particles in a hot plasma, and then apply them by solving for the physics of various geometries. Afterward, I stood at a white board before three professors from my department, answering their questions about the underlying physics behind the laser polarimeter I was building for my research project.

I remember leaving the exams exhausted, painfully aware of my mistakes, proud of the effort I had put in, but with no idea about the outcome. Later, I was pulled aside by one of the faculty and told that I had not passed.

It was devastating. Never in my life had I tried my absolute hardest. To put my full self into this endeavor, to hold myself up for evaluation, felt terrifying. And then to fail? I didn't know what to do with the pain. I yelled into the night as I walked home along Albany Street. I cried. All that effort, over all that time, and all for naught. It felt like I was making zero progress, and the only possible explanation was that I simply lacked the intelligence. I must be stupid, broken, worthless. I didn't even dare think about the implications of this on my future, which felt pretty bleak and hopeless.

I share this story without a filter, hoping that it can help you if you ever feel this kind of discouragement. There's no way to sugarcoat it. Failure is simply hard, and it's all the more challenging when you have put a lot in. Later I realized that my very identity had been on the line—as a smart person, as a good student, as a winner. I felt like I lost everything.

But now I have lived the rest of the story, learning first-hand the lesson of looking backward to notice the progress you have made. After failing my exams (and spending some time in mourning), I set to work on my classes and research, knowing I would have another opportunity in a year to take them again. I was determined to overcome it.

At the same time, I began to question whether the academic track was right for me. I met with a guidance counselor. I read about careers. I took quizzes. My investigation led me to a string of phone calls with strangers, mostly MIT alumni who had gone on to the "real world" of careers outside the university. These people were amazingly generous, willing to set aside valuable time, learn about a grad student with an identity crisis, ask thoughtful questions, and offer heartfelt advice. I've tried to pay that one forward, but I still feel in debt for this gift at a time I really needed it.

In all these phone calls, I learned a lot about career tracks, the worlds of business and engineering and consulting, and the skill sets that would help me as I exited academia. More than any of this, though, I learned about myself. These unbiased observers were able to see things in me that I couldn't see, and they had no reservations about communicating directly. Some were pleasant, some were gruff, but the composite result was a mirror held up so I could understand myself. And guess what I found? I saw progress. I understood the commercial value of the skills and techniques I had spent years building. I realized the contribution I was capable of, through my natural abilities and determined effort.

These observations would become concrete for me over years of working in the business world. But at the time, they were exactly what I needed in order to pick myself up, dust myself off, and move forward. It was like a group of strangers helping me turn around and see the progress I had been making.

You can do the same thing, especially in challenging moments. Pause, reflect, write down your observations. Turn to people you trust, whether you've known them for years or minutes. Look backwards, and you'll see the progress you've already made. Then, keep walking forward, because there is so much more in store.

That's all I have for warnings and advice. I hope you find some of this useful, whether now or in the future as you continue your journey as an empowered learner. As you climb mountains of your own, you'll collect your own warnings and advice to share with your fellow learners.

# Conclusion

THANK YOU FOR JOINING ME ON THIS EXPLORATION OF LEARNING. As you explore the beliefs and habits that empowered learners use to achieve great things, you are lighting a fire for yourself and everyone around you.

Remember the Plutarch quote?

"The mind is not a vessel to be filled, but a fire to be kindled."

I believe kindling a fire in the human mind is the most important thing we can do. I believe human beings have the capacity to solve all of our problems and prosper together in ways we can hardly conceive. I believe that starts with a shift in our thinking and a strong commitment to learning.

This is the conclusion of the book, but it should feel like a beginning as well. I hope you will decide to be an empowered learner. I hope you will bring it into your workplace and your hobbies and your personal relationships. I believe the ideas in this book will help you find real power, the kind that makes lasting change for you and everyone around you. The five core values will help you in your quest.

## A Moment in History

On the night of October 4, 1957, American families looked at the night sky and saw a shining dot streak past the stars. It was a Russian satellite called Sputnik, the first manmade object to orbit the Earth. Technologically, that's pretty cool. But it was also scary. Americans worried that they were losing in math, science, and engineering. With the Cold War in full swing, people feared that Russia could drop nuclear bombs from space. Americans were digging bomb shelters, stockpiling supplies, and practicing "duck and cover" drills.

But something else happened as a response to this moment. Learning took on a new importance. Schoolchildren heard an impassioned invitation from the President of the United States: your country needs you. Scientists and engineers tackled challenging problems with renewed resolve. Children and adults accepted the challenge, and the results were astonishing. The percentage of college students focusing on science and engineering nearly doubled in a very short time frame. Many new technologies were invented, including GPS and CAT scans.

That was 1957, but there is a direct parallel to the present moment. Individuals, families, and society as a whole have grappled with forces impacting the world, coming at us with high speed and daunting magnitude. In the last few years, a global pandemic has impacted all of us, placing additional strain on societal dysfunction and institutional breakdowns that have been building for decades.

It's clear that humanity will face tricky problems over the next fifty years. Climate, health, natural disasters, inequality, economic decline, political instability—the list goes on and on. The problems can barely be articulated right now, much less the solutions. And many of the tools, techniques, and other building blocks that will be part of these solutions have not been invented yet!

By now, you might agree, it's not enough to steer kids into biotech majors. It's not enough to ask math questions on a state exam. It's not enough to settle for cramming and regurgitating facts. By now, you probably understand where I'm coming from on this. To overcome our future challenges, we need a generation of learners.

We need people who make a deliberate choice to learn new things, then get to work with the mindset, skills, and habits of powerful learning. We need more good questions. We need more audacious goals. We need more humility and courage and persistence and confidence.

We need people who understand themselves and build on that understanding to make their unique contribution. We need people who see learning as a team sport and generously support everyone around them. We need people who refuse to give up on a life of progress and growth, who dare to be empowered learners.

Did I mention that it's fun to be a learner? It opens the door to a steady flow of new people and new experiences. It satisfies something deep in the human spirit. It is the only way to become the person you really want to be. It's critical to our future as a species.

Your invitation—right now—is to choose to be a learner. The last seven chapters have laid the case. We've talked about what it means to choose learning, and how learning includes so much more than memorizing facts for a multiple-choice test. In every case, real, powerful learning starts with a deliberate decision: asking a question, setting a goal, engaging with another person.

How would your life be different if learning was the goal? What would you try? Where would you go? What would you create?

What could you contribute to the people around you by becoming an empowered learner? How could your unique gifts have an impact? How would your family be different if you made it a quest to support the learning of your loved ones? What about your neighborhood? Your city? The world?

These are challenging, personal, lofty questions. One way to tackle them is to start with the end in mind.

## The End in Mind

One of the very first projects in my inaugural microschool was a little morbid. I asked the students to imagine a date years in the future, after they had lived a full, happy life, when their loved ones were gathered for their funeral. The task was to write the eulogy, crafting the story of their life they would want told, all those years in the future. It was fascinating to read their speeches, filled with silly jokes to heartfelt memories to sincere aspirations.

Thinking this way uncovers fascinating insights. The process forces you to consider life with a fresh perspective; after all, you are writing about a life that has yet to be lived. You're creating a story from scratch, and you are the one who will decide what happens. To borrow one of Stephen Covey's *7 Habits of Highly Effective People*, this exercise forces you to "begin with the end in mind."[55]

The idea is to get as clear as you can about the future you'd like to achieve. I like the funeral speech as the perfect forcing function, because contemplating death reveals your true priorities in a way nothing else can.

What would you want said about you in your eulogy? Take a moment to go there in your mind. What life did you build? What type of person have you become? What have you tried? What have you learned? What have you accomplished?

If you're like me, this exercise is daunting, even overwhelming, because the person I want to become is quite different than the one I see in the mirror every day. Changing from current to future me will require effort and it will entail setbacks. It will require new skills, new information, new friends. In a word, it will require learning.

My hope for you is that you will make a deliberate choice to be a learner, that you will build the mindsets and skills from this

[55] Stephen R. Covey, *The 7 Habits of Highly Effective People: Powerful Lessons in Personal Change* (New York: Simon & Schuster, 2013), 105.

book and apply them to the mountains you climb. I hope you'll stick with it, even when learning is uncomfortable. I hope you will experience the thrill of kindling a fire in your own mind, in your life, and in the world around you.

Are you ready to be an empowered learner? Let's get started.